MW00528884

Rules to Riches

Rules to Riches

Eight Simple Strategies That Will
Catapult You to Financial Security

Mark Baird

In preparation of this book every effort has been made to provide current and accurate information about personal finances. Nonetheless, inadvertent errors can occur and rules regarding tax, and other financial matters can and do change. This book is meant to be used for general education purposes and should not be interpreted as individual advice. If specific legal, accounting, tax, investment, real estate or other expert advice is needed or appropriate, the reader is strongly encouraged to obtain the services of a qualified professional expert with regard to the reader's specific situation. The author will not be responsible for any liability, loss, or risk experienced from the use of any of the information contained in this book.

COPYRIGHT © 2017 MARK BAIRD
All rights reserved.

RULES TO RICHES
Eight Simple Strategies That Will Catapult You to Financial Security

ISBN   978-1-61961-584-7 *Paperback*
       978-1-61961-585-4 *Ebook*

LIONCREST
PUBLISHING

To my sons, Joshua and Jacob. They are the inspiration for this book, as is giving them a written record for all the spoken words that they may be tired of hearing but that are still true. Now you have no excuse!

Contents

Foreword

BY C. DEAN WOODS

So, why another book about financial planning? If you've visited a bookstore recently, I'm fairly certain you would have seen an entire section dedicated to the subject. My favorite bookstore has a couple of hundred titles in their section, with some authors penning multiple volumes on the subject. I can only think of one reason we need another book whose objective is to educate our citizenry on how they can create financial freedom for themselves. And that reason is? So far, not much is working very well. And why? In my view, there are two reasons. First, it's human nature to choose immediate gratification over saving for the future. Second, saving for the future is difficult. It's very hard to picture what our needs will be during retirement, but it's easy to see what they are now. And most of those needs have to be met now with cold, hard cash.

The results? Too many retired Americans are *not* living the dream and are struggling financially. This should not be. But the facts paint a very stark picture. It's an absolute fact that too many people enter retirement with little or no savings, and most younger Americans aren't doing much to ensure their financial future.

Skeptical? When you get a chance, go to your computer and put the following phrase into your search engine: *financial status of retired Americans.* Then click on any of the resulting articles, and see for yourself. If the statistics and facts shown in these articles don't give you a wake-up call, hopefully Mark's book will.

Speaking of Mark, I would chalk up the reason why reading his take on financial planning will serve you well to, not only his training and experience, but his heart and spirit. His passion for helping people secure their financial future will be evident to you as you read his insightful thoughts on a subject that can be quite complex. So, who is this man?

I first met Mark in 1998 at the Fortune 500 company we both worked for in Houston, Texas. I was the head of benefits at the time, and we had just concluded the consolidation of three separate benefits programs into one after a merger. As we began to deal with the myriad of issues communicating and managing the new program, we soon learned how difficult it was going to be to manage the expectations of over ten thousand employees, many of whom were in very skeptical bargaining units, and all of whom were quite concerned about their new benefit package. They were concerned, you see, because we had changed the traditional final average pension plans these employees had become accustomed to, and relied on for much of their future financial security, to a cash-balance style plan (a relatively new design being slowly accepted throughout corporate America—a plan they had little understanding of and certainly no trust in). While we had endeavored to ensure that the new pension plan design, along with an enhanced 401(k) savings plan to go along with it, would still meet the financial security needs of our evolving employee group, we concluded it was imperative that we better educate our employees about how to maximize the value of these two financial security plans. So, we sought to find someone with a financial-planning background, who could not only grasp how these new plans worked and why they were being implemented, but who could, most importantly, speak the language of our employees and hopefully gain their trust. And that person turned out to be Mark Baird, a corn farmer from Indiana.

Mark, after leaving his family's successful farming venture, joined our company and served in various roles for several years, and in his spare time he studied for and obtained his CERTIFIED FINANCIAL PLANNER™ certification. Even though Mark had no experience working in a human resources or benefits department, he won the job because he convinced us that he had the capability to effectively communicate to our employees, primarily based on his knowledge and passion for the task. Before seeking the position, Mark did his homework, and he already knew the details of our new plans, as well as the objectives we were hoping to achieve with them. After working within the company for several years, he came to know our employees very well, and he knew how to speak their language. Long story short, Mark's work in those early years was instrumental in gaining our employees' trust and their ultimate acceptance of the new plans. What he did for our employees, he can do for you.

So, let me urge you not to put this book down until you have taken the time to absorb what Mark has so painstakingly composed. If you will do that, and then follow through and apply the principles he outlines for you, I am confident you will achieve that sound financial future you deserve. Good luck and good planning.

—C. DEAN WOODS
FORMER SR. VICE PRESIDENT AND CHIEF HUMAN
RESOURCES OFFICER, CENTERPOINT ENERGY

Introduction

ONE ROCK AT A TIME

I grew up on a farm in Indiana where there was always something that needed to be done. There were the typical jobs one associates with farm life—feeding the animals, tilling the soil, hoeing weeds. There also were a few tasks non-farm dwellers might find strange, including one of my first jobs. For years, my main responsibility was picking up rocks from a two-hundred-acre field.

I am not referring to tiny, easy-to-grab pebbles. I am referring to rocks the size of your fist and larger. Some were the size of a rather large pumpkin; some were as big as a car. Our farm was located in a flat former swampland that was drained by the backbreaking labor of its settlers. Prior to that, glaciers covered the area, and as they receded, they acted like bulldozers, scraping the top of the earth flat and depositing rocks and boulders along the way.

Rocks are destroyers of farming equipment, especially combine harvesters. A new machine can cost well over $400,000. A large rock ripping through its guts can result in costly repairs and, worse, a delayed harvest. To rid the land of these threats to your income, you need two pieces of equipment: a tractor with a front-end loader and a shovel. More importantly, you need a plan. You need to know where you plan to start and stop. You need to be flexible and ready for surprises. You might run into a rock so big you can't move it alone. You might come across a bonus—an Indian arrowhead! In every case, you have to persevere, use your best judgment, and have a plan of attack.

Before the advent of heavy equipment, early settlers used horses, mules, and strong backs to attack these rocks. One other resource proved invaluable when the rocks were too large for lifting—dynamite. The force of the explosion would split the rocks into a more manageable size. Knowing this, a neighbor of ours once opted for this solution when he encountered his own immovable mass. Using his limited knowledge of explosives, he dug several holes around the bottom of the huge rock, packed the holes with several sticks of dynamite, lit the fuse, and stood back. As expected, the explosion had a significant impact on the rock—just not the impact he predicted. What our neighbor failed to remember was that the dynamite should have been packed on top of the rock, forcing the explosive impact downward to split it in two. When you pack dynamite under a rock, the dynamite explodes and shoots the rock several feet up into the air, after which the rock simply falls back to the ground into a deeper hole. The moral of the story is this: Get someone with experience to help if you have heavy lifting to do.

For me, picking up rocks has long been a metaphor for life. Just like the obstacles we all face, rocks come in different shapes and sizes. Some can be picked up with one hand and carried to a proper resting place. Others require more effort and planning. You might have to ask for help from others to pry it out of its hole. You might have to bring in some equipment to do the heavy lifting. You might even need to blow it up into tiny pieces to make things more manageable. No matter how monumental the task, you do it by making a plan and then picking up one rock at a time. The same is true of achieving financial success. You do it with a plan and action, step by step.

You have picked up this book for a reason. Perhaps you have a sinking feeling that the way you handle your money is not really working. Perhaps you are worried your approach won't work for the long haul. Maybe you have recently inherited wealth. Maybe you have no wealth at all. Maybe you want to be generous, and "stuff" is getting in your way.

Regardless of your reason, by simply opening this book you have taken a step in the right direction toward learning more about your personal finances. This book is a call to action. Through these pages, I hope to give you the confidence to embark on a clearer financial journey.

We all like to believe attaining wealth has to be complicated. We assume one needs a great amount of knowledge to propel himself to millionaire status. This is not the case. Financial riches can be cultivated merely by employing a few simple rules. I call these the "Rules to Riches." You may be skeptical, but I can assure you that if you follow the rules, make a plan, and consistently work the plan, you will be rich beyond your wildest dreams.

Building wealth is more about behavior than knowledge, and showing hardworking people the path toward successful decision-making is one of my motivations for writing this book. Some of the rules may seem surprising, perhaps even counter to conventional wisdom. Some are plain old common sense but can be tougher than they seem to implement. Some require seeking outside help, which many of us are reluctant to do.

My biggest motivation for writing runs deeper than simply helping you build wealth. I want to give you the knowledge you need to get off the runaway train of consumption and consumer debt. That train only has one stop: a place of anxiety, stress, and the feeling of being trapped.

Most of us have an innate desire to be financially successful, no matter our lot in life. Yet many of us also believe becoming rich is beyond our reach, and we are daily bombarded with statistics to further our frustrations. The numbers are staggering. For instance, 70 percent of Americans live paycheck to paycheck regardless of income level. It may not be apparent as we drive up and down the streets of suburbia or the inner city, but the average American has credit-card debt around $15,000, the bulk of which did not come from big expenses. It came from trips to the grocery store or Target or Walmart and accumulated over time. As a whole, Americans have over a trillion dollars in credit-card debt. On top of that, each of us with a car loan has an average outstanding debt of over $26,000. Add to that student-loan debt—an average of $47,000 among those who have such debt—and escaping debt's clenches begins to seem impossible. I can help you eliminate the debt weighing you down.

Make no mistake, despite this book's title, I am a firm believer that one does not have to be monetarily rich to live rich. I believe many of us place so much importance on earthly riches that we lose sight of our relationships, experiences, and the need to help others—the things that really matter most. We become so focused on the here and now that we forget we take nothing with us when we leave this life. We ignore the value of the intangible things that enrich our lives that far exceed anything money can buy.

Two of my favorite quotations best sum up what money really means. The runner Steve Scott once said, "Happiness is not bought by money, but it can buy circumstances and conditions that improve the chances of a worldly kind of happiness." In other words, money is not the end but a means to the end, and we all must decide what goals matter most to us individually. We all measure financial success differently. Noted salesman and motivational speaker Zig Ziglar said, "Money isn't the most important thing in life, but it's reasonably close to oxygen on the 'Gotta Have It' scale"—again, money is not the final end game but sustenance to get us there.

Becoming a financially sound person requires a certain set of traits and characteristics. A good place to start is by living within your means and never spending more than your income. Such an idea is easier said than done, but this book will prove it's not as hard as you might think. Next, it's important to define your goals and objectives and work toward them, all the while adjusting your outlook as life happens. Because, as we all know, life always happens. Planning for unforeseen circumstances is crucial. From a car breaking down or a roof needing replacing to the loss of a job or untimely death, there are countless ways our plans can be disrupted. Having a sufficient way to address these events is critical. Finally, it is an absolute necessity to have a plan for when you leave this world. None of us are going to escape this place alive. Why not make the lives of our loved ones less stressful by having an adequate plan in place for when the inevitable occurs?

A financially sound person has an overall comprehensive plan weaving all these things together, yet there are surprisingly few people who have taken the time to create one. Some incorrectly assume that if they are of a certain age, it is too late to even consider getting started. While it might be easier and ultimately more beneficial to start when you are age twenty, it is never too late to take the first steps toward improving your situation.

Think of your financial plan as being like a road map: it will get you from where you are to where you're going, wherever that might be. Just like we wouldn't expect our gut to guide us to a strange address in a far-off city without

GPS telling us where to turn, we shouldn't expect our intuition to miraculously get us to our financial goals.

There are many books written on personal finance and even more websites and blogs whose writers claim to be "experts." Most of them are well-meaning people sharing good information. The biggest problem is much of this information is given in isolation. The writers tend to give simplistic answers to complex problems because they lack the in-depth education or training necessary to give informed and qualified advice. If you decide to embark on your journey toward financial freedom on your own without outside help from a financial advisor, I suggest educating yourself as best you can. If you do seek out someone for advice, be sure that person is qualified to dig into the weeds of your particular situation. While the Internet is helpful in many ways, it cannot provide the personal connection required to navigate each person's unique financial situation. It's impossible for a robo-advisor to know you as well as a real, living human being.

The approach I will lay out for you in this book works where others fail because it is interactive and fueled by your own motivation. Procrastination and failure to act are the enemies, and in my field of financial advising, I see quite a bit. I've met with countless numbers of people who know they have a problem but choose to ignore it. It's human nature to avoid the things we don't understand or like, whether it's doing the dishes, or mowing the yard, or cleaning the litter box. But when we avoid things we don't want to face, the problem only worsens.

When it comes to finances, people don't want to look at their credit-card statement or at how deeply in debt they are. This is where accountability becomes key. We need something other than an alert on a phone or a machine telling us we need to check in. We need someone other than ourselves, whether it's a spouse, financial advisor, or trusted friend, to make sure we're staying on track. An app is not enough. The electronic world of financial monitoring can be great, but in some cases, it becomes a crutch. People think because they are using something such as Quicken or Mint or receiving digital alerts concerning their credit cards, they are engaged in their finances. In reality, these tools have eliminated the need for face-to-face, one-on-one interaction. Sometimes, a physical conversation needs to take place. We need the ability to interject and ask questions rather than just filling out a questionnaire online.

In order to truly get control over your financial life, you have to be purposeful in seeking out help. It is not easy initially. It takes a lot of time, but the work is worth it to both you and your family, especially in situations where one person is the primary financial mind of the house. If something were to happen to that person, the spouse would be lost and dependent on people he or she has never met. Establishing a relationship early with an accountability partner can lessen the stress in an already difficult situation.

The benefits of having a plan stretch far beyond times of immediate crisis. My peers and I joke that sometimes we're more in the marriage-counseling business than the money-management business. It's no secret that money is the number-one cause of failed marriages. Early on in my counseling business, I was affiliated with a financial-coaching website. If someone was in need of help beyond what the site offered, he or she reached out to me. Scrolling through some of the requests can show just how much trouble real people are in. Some are couples who have been married decades, and they just can't seem to reach financial stability. Some are expectant parents who are looking at their future with concern. They all are struggling with debt, which is causing a rift in the relationship, affecting their kids and compromising everyone's well-being.

Largely, the fault for so many of us finding ourselves in these situations falls to the nature of our consumer society. Marketers do a fantastic job of convincing us we always need the next best thing. We are never satisfied—we always need the newer car, the bigger house, the flashier lifestyle. To buy those things we want but don't necessarily need requires a financial wherewithal that many of us are told we have, but lack in reality.

We need self-discipline and mindfulness, traits anyone can learn, to guide us in these matters. I believe everyone should be required to take a course in personal financial management a couple of years after high school or college when they are earning money and trying to make ends meet. It would certainly save a lot of headaches down the road. Discipline is not something most people are born with, and managing money requires it. In order to be disciplined about money, you have to have a plan. Even if we fear what the plan might show us, we have to go through the process in order to obtain financial security.

In the pages of this book, you will learn exactly how to develop such a plan. Each chapter is based on one of the Eight Rules to Riches. Each addresses a specific area of personal finance and offers guidance for creating your own road map to success—from what to do when you're just starting out to how to plan for retirement. If developing a household budget is your goal, pay special attention to Rule 2, "Know and Direct Your Dollars." Rule 5, "Curb Your Enthusiasm," offers guidance for anyone looking to buy a house, and Rule 6, "Save, Invest, and Save Some More," focuses on retirement savings. Many have helpful charts and sidebars to get you started on your own journey toward financial health. They also are available online at the website created for this book, RulesToRiches.com.

No matter where you are in your life, it is not too late to begin thinking about your finances. The important thing is to start now. You will avoid regret if you start with a plan of attack and go rock by rock—or in this case, rule by rule.

Rule One

CREATE A COMPREHENSIVE FINANCIAL PLAN

"Plans fail for lack of counsel, but with many advisors they succeed."

—PROVERBS 15:22

It's best if I just get this out of the way right up-front: financial planning is not sexy. Even I, a man who has made his life out of helping others create their own financial plans, hate doing it for myself. I prefer to live in the moment, doing what I want to do when I want to do it and spending what I want to spend when I want to spend it. But I learned a long time ago that such behavior does not serve me nor my family well. It leads to strife, uncertainty, arguments, and hurt feelings. Making a financial plan and keeping it current will be one of the most important gifts you can give yourself and your family.

Anyone can make a plan, regardless of income level. How many times have we heard stories of people of seemingly meager means who pass away and leave huge sums of money to churches or charities? In each instance, we ask, "How were they possibly able to do it?" The answer is simple: They had a plan. Even if they didn't have a formal plan, they were intentional about their financial life. They had at least a cursory understanding of investing. It truly doesn't matter whether you make $25,000 a year or $250,000 a year—everyone can reach their goals. It might take some people longer than others, but managing our finances and being good stewards of all that we have is key to being successful.

We are all called to be financially responsible citizens, not just for ourselves but for the benefit of our families. Many people try to escape responsibility and accountability without a clear picture of the day of reckoning. When times get tough, they want to declare bankruptcy, essentially giving up before they even know what they do or don't have. Many times, we act on what we think we know is the truth, but it's not. It takes more than just our own understanding to figure things out. Lack of knowledge or unwise financial decisions are not things to be ashamed of—they simply force us to acknowledge that informed outside help is sometimes necessary. If your health is failing and you need an operation, you don't rely solely on a friend or the Internet to diagnose or treat your illness. You seek out a professional who knows the best course of action. Sifting through what that means for you often requires looking to others. Your financial health can have a profound impact on many different aspects of your life. Tap into the sources you need.

It also helps to think of managing your finances as an art, not a science. In the beginning, it requires a lot of flexibility. It also requires that you not be overly critical of yourself. You might not be happy with your previous habits, but that's why you're making changes now. Allow yourself the freedom to see things clearly and to realize this is a commitment to a new way of life. Think of it as being like losing weight: you don't do it overnight. You didn't get into financial difficulty overnight, and you're not going to get out of it that quickly either. Depending on your situation, it can take months or years, and that's okay.

I understand words like "budget" and "balance sheet" can make just about anybody want to take off running in the opposite direction. I encourage you to think of these less as things to be feared or loathed and more as tools capable of opening a world of possibility. People think "budgeting" means they will have to decrease their spending, and for most of us, that seems nearly impossible. In reality, budgeting does not necessarily mean cutting costs. A budget is nothing more than a tool telling your money where to go. A better term than budget is "cash management," because you really are managing the cash coming into and going out of your household.

A "balance sheet" is nothing more than a look at what you own and what you owe, which is why I call it an "owe/own sheet." It provides a snapshot of whether you are financially ahead or behind in life. What you own is called an "asset"—everything from your home to your car, jewelry, clothes, furniture, 401(k) investments, IRA investments, all of it. It is not your income. The flipside is debt, or what you owe, also known as a liability. If you own a house worth $150,000, you put that on the "asset" side. But let's say you have a mortgage on the property, and you have a $100,000 debt against it. That goes to the liability side. The liability minus the asset is $50,000. You're to the plus side with $50,000, though when it comes to real estate, numbers can flip based on market value, as many did during the housing crisis of 2009. We'll talk more about home ownership in chapter 5.

With a budget, every time money comes in, you decide

how to allocate it. To do so effectively, you have to look at your spending and see where your money goes every month. This part of the process is everyone's least favorite. No one wants to sit down and see every swipe of the debit card, every ATM withdrawal, every credit card purchase, but this is critical. Creation of a realistic plan depends on it.

As you go along, it's important to remember that there is no one plan perfect for everyone, as all families have different goals. Some want to pay off homes before retirement age. Others want to eliminate credit-card debt. Some want to save for a child's education or start a business. Regardless of its nature, every plan requires a goal. At this point, I encourage people to dream big. Nothing is impossible. If the church or charity you care about owes a million dollars and you want to help pay that off, write it down as a goal. As a possible solution, you could buy a life-insurance policy and name the church as a beneficiary. Maybe you want to retire at age fifty, or buy a vacation home, or travel the world. Dream your dreams, and don't hold back. Write it down, and figure out later how doable it is.

Finally, every plan needs to be revisited at least once a year. Things change in our lives that impact both our finances and our goals, so we need to reevaluate as frequently as necessary. Sometimes, that means taking money away from one expense so you can put it toward the things you really want. My family recently did this with our $130-a-month cable bill. The cost started to seem exorbitant for something we rarely use. We called the company and had our bill lowered to $60 a month. We don't have all the channels we previously had, but not having Turner Classic Movies is not the end of the world. Allow yourself to make adjustments to reach your goals. Life is not static, nor should our financial plans be.

WHAT'S THE PLAN?

The process starts with writing down what you own and what you owe. Some people will feel great after doing this. Some will not. At this point, that's not important. What's important is getting it down on paper.

Net Worth Calculator

ASSETS

Cash

Checking accounts	
Savings accounts	
CDs (certificates of deposit)	
Life Insurance (cash surrender value)	
Other cash	
Total Cash	

Investments

Securities (stocks, bonds, mutual funds)	
Treasury Bills	
Other investments	
Total Investments	

Property

Real Estate (market value)	
Automobile (present value)	
Bullion (silver, gold, etc)	
Jewelry, Art and Collectibles	
Other property	
Total Property	

Retirement

Retirements accounts (IRA, 401k)	
Estimated Employer Pensions ($/month*240)	
Estimated Social Security ($/month*240)	
Other assets	
Total Retirement	
Total Assets	

LIABILITIES

Accounts Payable	
Auto Loan	
Credit Card Debt	
Consumer Loans or Installments	
Loan on Life Insurance	
Real Estate Mortgages	
Student Loans	
Unpaid Taxes	
Money Owed to Others	
Other liabilities	
Total Liabilities	

Total Assets - Total Liabilities = Net Worth

This calculator appears courtesy of Vertex42.com and can be found at www.vertex42.com/ Calculators/net-worth.html and is also available at RulesToRiches.com

Start by subtracting what you owe from what you own to determine your net worth.

Next, evaluate your cash flow. Write down all your household expenses: groceries, electricity, cable TV, eating out. Show where every and any dollar goes. Go back as far as you can—a year preferably, but at least three months—to get an accurate picture of what you have. Get out get your checkbook register. Grab your credit-card and debit-card statements. Keep receipts for cash purchases. Write everything down. Consider one-time-a-year costs, such as insurance premiums. Track what you spend using the template. Your overall goal for this exercise is to account for every dollar and make sure that when you subtract inflows minus outflows the result is zero. If you have done it right, the result should not be a positive number. All your money goes somewhere, whether it's savings, debt retirement, or any other number of places. A positive number means you don't know where all your money is going. If this happens, don't despair. On average, most people can't account for 10 to 15 percent of their cash flow simply because they are not keeping close enough track of every dollar spent.

Yearly Budget Calculator

Note that this calculator appears courtesy of Vertex42.com and is abbreviated for the purposes of space. The full budget calculator can be found at www.vertex42.com/Calculators/budget-calculator.html

I know that, for some, this is not going to be fun. You might be left feeling angry at yourself or a spouse or even depressed. That's okay. At this point, you are getting an overall sense of your financial health. Owning more than you owe is good from a "net worth" standpoint but doesn't necessarily mean your cash flow is stable and organized. Spending less than your income is ideal, but you still must consider your goals and where you want to be one year from now, ten years from now, twenty years from now, and so on. Remember: There is no one-size-fits-all plan out there. You're creating your plan for you and your specific goals. The plan is meant to give you hope, and it will lead to the steps necessary to get you back on track. The plan forces you to stop assuming things about your finances and helps you see things truthfully, but no matter where you are financially, there are options and solutions.

It's important also to consider future obligations—in other words, plan for both the worst and the best possible scenarios. Even if you're not certain what will happen, you want to avoid any negative surprises. Perhaps you won't need all the money you save for the care of a parent, and you can redirect that to one of your goals. Maybe your child will get a scholarship, and tuition money can be used elsewhere. You might inherit money. All of these are things to consider in an annual review of your finances as you reshape your plan.

Oftentimes at this point, financial planners and tax professionals are able to find additional income-tax savings. For example, if the goal is to save for college, the planner might recommend a state-sponsored 529 plan. Some of these plans allow for state income-tax credits, leading to future savings. If the goal is to start a business, there are tax deductions planners can help you find. You can start a business out of almost anything. My family and I live in a house in a rural area with a large yard. After several years, I became tired of mowing grass. We plowed part of it and planted popcorn. At the time, I didn't know much about the ins and outs of popcorn growing or selling, but we forged ahead and turned it into a small family business. Now, we go to farmers' markets and sell popcorn. Starting a business is a great option for anyone nearing retirement who's not quite ready to fish all day. Figure out something you like to do, and do it. Whether it's one day a week or seven days a week, it allows you to take something you enjoy and turn it into something that benefits you and, hopefully, others. Read more about starting a business in chapter 7.

INVESTMENT: IS IT WORTH THE RISK?

There is no investment without risk, and it's important to establish what kind of risk you're willing to take. Even if you inherit wealth or win the lottery, you will have to take on some degree of risk in order to maintain or grow the wealth you already have. Putting all your money in the bank is one of the safest forms of investing, but it pays little more than simply sticking your cash under a mattress.

The key is to invest in things you understand over a long period of time. Don't get caught up in the latest trends. Diversify your investments. Look to longtime investors such as Warren Buffett, and learn from their experience as well as their mistakes. Buffett famously said, "Diversification is protection against ignorance. It makes little sense if you know what you are doing." You can own similar investments in similar classes, but you must do the homework. Having twenty different mutual funds doesn't mean you're diversified. You must look at the underlying investments. Be patient, and use common sense. You might, on occasion, hear someone brag about investing in a stock and watching it jump 50 percent overnight. We'd all love such a quick fix, and while you may be lucky enough to find one, they're not easy to come by and rarely pan out.

When deciding how to invest, it's important to consider your accumulation goals. Ask yourself what you want your money to do for you. Most of us live in the here and now and focus solely on taking care of "today," but I urge everyone to consider all their goals, short-term and long-term, from the very beginning. Even if you've just graduated college, think about the day, years from now, when you'll want to slow down and step away from a wage-paying job or a business you've created and helped grow. At that point, you'll likely need passive income. Start planning for that day now.

Your accumulation goals depend on the phase of life you are in. Your goals can and will change as your life progresses, but all will require saving. A Savings Goal Tracker gives examples of the different goals one might have. Categories include home repair, vehicle replacement, an emergency fund, vacation, and Christmas gifts. This can be altered to reflect any goal and allows you to monitor how you're saving for each. It functions as a reminder of your financial needs and helps you see beyond the immediate present.

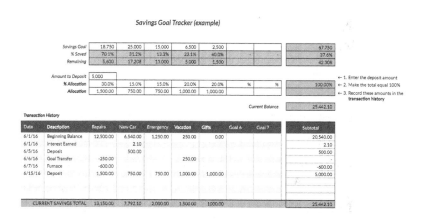

Savings Goal Tracker (example)

Savings Goal	18,750	25,000	15,000	6,500	2,500			67,750
% Saved	70.1%	31.2%	13.3%	23.1%	40.0%	-	-	37.6%
Remaining	5,600	17,208	13,000	5,000	1,500			42,308

Amount to Deposit	5,000							
% Allocation	30.0%	15.0%	15.0%	20.0%	20.0%	%	%	100.00%
Allocation	1,500.00	750.00	750.00	1,000.00	1,000.00			

← 1. Enter the deposit amount
← 2. Make the total equal 100%
← 3. Record these amounts in the transaction history

Current Balance 25,442.10

Transaction History

Date	Description	Repairs	New Car	Emergency	Vacation	Gifts	Goal 6	Goal 7	Subtotal
6/1/16	Beginning Balance	12,500.00	6,540.00	1,250.00	250.00	0.00			20,540.00
6/1/16	Interest Earned		2.10						2.10
6/5/16	Deposit		500.00						500.00
6/6/16	Goal Transfer	-250.00			250.00				
6/7/16	Furnace	-600.00							-600.00
6/15/16	Deposit	1,500.00	750.00	750.00	1,000.00	1,000.00			5,000.00
CURRENT SAVINGS TOTAL		13,150.00	7,792.10	2,000.00	1,500.00	1000.00			25,442.10

This calculator appears courtesy of Vertex42.com and can be found at www.vertex42.com/ExcelTemplates/savings-goal-tracker.html

Anticipating needs helps us avoid falling back on debt when life's inconveniences—a roof needing replacement, a vehicle dying, or a hot water tank breaking—inevitably occur. The beginning of your career is the ideal time to begin thinking this way. People who are toward the end of a career often are dealing with the cleanup of poor financial decisions. Perhaps, rather than saving, they went into debt or took out a home equity loan for home repairs. They might be burdened with large car loans even as they approach retirement. Anticipating these things early in life helps you focus on what you truly desire rather than spending frivolously or on impulse.

Failure to have a handle on risk, future needs, and our passions can lead to worry, stress, and a less than enjoyable retirement. I've known people who retire early with an unreasonable expectation on passive income from pensions and interest. Many times, they've listened to so-called experts, maybe even radio pundits or seminar presenters, who tell them they can expect 10 to 12 percent returns from the stock market, through mutual funds, or through some other returns from exotic investments. Like the old adage warns, "If it sounds too good to be true, then it is." As you approach retirement, the risk associated with your investments should be reduced.

ARE YOU COVERED?

Risk management is something everyone should consider. The term "risk management" is really a fancy word for insurance coverage, but agents prefer it because the word "insurance" carries a bad connotation. Limiting risk can improve our wealth, whereas one catastrophic accident or event can lead to a huge financial hit. Insurance is something few of us like to think about, unless you sell it. It's one of those products you buy and hope you never need. Some of us ignore the need, rolling the dice day by day, yet everyone needs insurance, no exception.

Some insurance is more important than others. Most of us have a need for life insurance for at least a portion of our lives, but not necessarily our entire lives. The death of a breadwinner can create a catastrophic situation for a family, and coverage through the workplace is only good as long as the recipient is working there. Replacing that breadwinner's income needs to be a priority. No one wants to think of that, but ignoring it can make a terrible situation even more stressful.

Once you know what kind of insurance you need, you must make sure you have enough of it. For example, assume you were to get a job paying $50,000 a year, and your employer offers you group term insurance at one to six times your salary. That's not enough for a young person with a family. A single person might not need more than that, but as a rule of thumb, if you are a couple with children, you'll need eight to ten times the main breadwinner's income in the event of untimely death. There also is the risk that if you leave that job, the coverage likely is not transferable.

If you're having health issues by the time you exit that

job, you would most certainly have to pay a higher rate than what you did under a group plan. One of the most cost-effective ways to ensure you have adequate life insurance is to get it when you're young and healthy. Term insurance is cheap, but as the name implies, it is only for a term. If your need for insurance continues, other forms of insurance should be investigated, such as guaranteed renewable term, universal life, and even whole life in some cases. If you reach the point when you need insurance and you're uninsurable on a new policy, you'll be thankful you considered these other options. Buying term insurance and investing the difference between it and a whole life product is an option if you have the time and discipline, but if you're young and no longer insurable, you could run out of time. I've seen situations where people become ill and simply can't buy cheap term insurance or any kind of life insurance. Had they bought a reasonable, universal life renewable term policy when they started working, their medical needs would not affect their ability to keep it.

When it comes to insurance for the home, everyone needs both the contents and the structure itself covered—and don't forget flood insurance. Many people are surprised when their homeowner's insurance doesn't cover damage from "rising water," which means flood water coming in from the outside. Damage from floods can have devastating effects. Depending on where you live, policies can be cheap or very expensive. Regardless, you cannot afford to be without one if you live in an area prone to flooding. Renters aren't immune to the effects of such damage. They also need coverage for their contents, from flood or fire or storm or burglary. These are all events most of us could ill afford to insure on our own, and making sure you have adequate coverage is all a part of the planning process.

The same applies to automobile insurance. Most states, if not all, have minimum coverage requirements from a liability standpoint. It's up to you to decide if you absolutely need full coverage for a vehicle that's been paid for. If a car is more than ten years old and worth only a few thousand dollars, full coverage is likely not worth the cost. At that point, it's smarter to self-insure and save what you would have paid for collision insurance in an emergency fund. Whatever plan you choose, make sure it covers you in the event you are hit by an uninsured driver. The liability limits required by states are often low. In these cases, I encourage people to look at the higher limits.

An umbrella policy provides coverage beyond the regular limits of homeowners and automobile policies, and most people do need one. With claims and jury awards at record levels, umbrella policies can cover you up to a higher limit than your other policies. For a basic policy, a $1,000,000 umbrella would cover you up to that amount. For instance, assume you were at fault for a car accident and the damages were $800,000. If the liability limits of your auto policy were $300,000, the umbrella would kick in and pay the difference of $500,000. Without an umbrella, you are responsible for the $500,000. An umbrella policy is relatively cheap compared to the large financial loss you would potentially have to endure.

I also encourage everyone to consider disability insurance. We are much more likely to be rendered unable to work because of injury or illness than we are to die prematurely. If you're covered by a disability policy at work, those premiums should be paid with after-tax dollars to ensure the benefit comes to you tax-free. Most policies cover at least half of your salary. Costs of assisted living or in-home nursing care can have a devastating impact on the size of an estate very quickly. The average cost of staying in a nursing home in the United States is $60,000 to $80,000 a year. Medicaid can pay for a portion of that, but your net worth has to be very low in order to qualify. If you're self-employed, look into an individual policy. Depending on your occupation, the cost can be very reasonable. As with any insurance policy, read the fine print. Disability policies can have many exclusions and hurdles to cross before benefits are paid. An insurance professional can guide you through the process.

Depending on your net worth, you may or may not need

long-term care insurance. If you have a family history that indicates you will require long-term care, it's wise to consider it at a younger age instead of waiting until your late fifties. The longer you wait, the more expensive it is. You'll pay for it longer, but your premiums will be lower.

Medical insurance is pretty much a necessity. The Affordable Care Act has made medical insurance available to everyone, although premiums and deductibles may be extremely expensive. My sense is that changes will be made to the program, but it's likely these changes won't result in lower costs. Employer plans are typically the best option, but costs for these are increasing, just as all medical insurance products and deductibles and benefits are becoming less generous. Bottom line: Do your homework—medical insurance is changing, and you have to be an informed consumer.

For most of us, once we turn sixty-five, Medicare becomes our primary medical insurance. Relying on Medicare alone is dangerous, as we're beginning to see the benefits of the system diminishing. The government is cutting the reimbursement rates for doctors and hospitals, which means people are paying more out-of-pocket than they ever have prior. This makes supplemental Medicare insurance critical, and there are many different variations. Be sure you and your planner are investigating the best options for you.

Another rising concern is identity theft, and protecting yourself from it is becoming increasingly important. If you're trying to buy a house or a car and somebody has tapped into your credit, it can create a huge mess. Several identity-protection insurance providers will do more than simply monitor your credit—they will help you clean it up. Costs can range from $100 to $500 a year, depending on the particular services they offer. Find the one that's best for you, and avoid the headache altogether.

ARE YOUR AFFAIRS IN ORDER?

Everyone needs a will. Fewer than half of the adult population have them, and those who do rarely update them. We've all heard people say, "Well, I don't care. I'll be dead and gone, and it won't matter." It indeed does matter greatly to the people who are left behind. You must ask yourself how you want your assets to be distributed. If you don't, the government will do it for you.

In addition, everyone needs to leave certain medical directives addressing how they want end-of-life scenarios to be handled. Do you want life-extending procedures to take place or not? Do you have documents in place that allow a trusted loved one or friend to advocate on your behalf or to sign documents on your behalf? Who is your power of attorney? If you are incapacitated, who has access to accounts for which you are the sole signer? What about online social accounts such as Facebook, Twitter, and LinkedIn? Without answers to these questions, you are putting your loved ones in highly stressful situations.

Everyone should have a minimum of four estate documents: a will; powers of attorney, both health-care and financial directive; and a spreadsheet detailing the locations of all your accounts and their required passwords so, in the event you are incapacitated, your family can access them. Put these all in a three-ring binder, and store it in a safe space such as a lock box and tell a loved one where it is.

You may also want to investigate online tools like Everplan that can be a tremendous aid in organizing information and documents if you become incapacitated.

Estate plans need to be updated at minimum after each significant life event, including but not limited to the birth of a child, a child becoming an adult, a divorce, or changing jobs. I recommend clients do a yearly checkup. Consider all that has changed in your life. What new things are going on? How are your parents? How are they being taken care of? Do you expect some sort of an inheritance? Has your financial condition changed? Most people with wills don't check them on a regular basis, and many have been made when their children were minors. As your life changes, so should your estate plan.

WHO CAN YOU TRUST?

Implementation of the plan by either you or your planner also should be ongoing. Some planners will both write a plan and implement it for the client with the help of an attorney, should one be required. You can opt to do it on your own, though in my experience, most people aren't as thorough when they choose that route. After reading this book, you should know the basic elements contained in a plan and the things to consider in order to build one well. You can do your own further research on the best insurance to buy for your particular situation and the best stocks or mutual funds to own, all of which are elements of a comprehensive plan.

Having a "do it myself" attitude is how my own journey in the financial-planning realm began. I loved the material and decided to take the same coursework that a financial planner takes in order to become a CERTIFIED FINANCIAL PLANNER™. I passed the required exams, then went on to complete other licensing requirements. I ended up working as the director of benefits for a Fortune 500 company and speaking to employees individually as well as in large groups.

I quickly discovered that our employees didn't really understand their benefits and, sometimes sadly, didn't understand their financial situations at all. Many thought they knew how their plans worked and believed that simply listening to what friends, family, and coworkers said about saving and investing would carry them to successful retirement. Most of the time, they were wrong. As Mark Twain said, "It ain't what you don't know that gets you in trouble. It's what you know for sure that just ain't so." We all suffer from this. We read an article or a blog or Facebook post and believe we now know everything we need to know. I call this "Instant Expert Syndrome." Sometimes, we have to admit that we don't have all the answers and seek help from those who know better.

Vetting the right financial planner requires an interview process just like hiring a candidate for any job or finding the right doctor that fits your needs. The first appointment is typically when that interview occurs, whether it's formal or informal. If you don't like the vibes you get from him or her, go on to the next. If the planner doesn't answer your questions as you think he or she should, move on. No one is going to be a better advocate for you than you. You will know best who is the right person to help you put your plan in motion.

When choosing a financial planner, look for someone who

is an excellent communicator, motivator, and accountability partner. More than just a financial planner, we need a financial coach. Much like a football coach, the planner sees the whole field. He plans plays and makes the most out of the strengths of his players. He lays out different scenarios that may or may not happen in every game, but he knows what adjustments might be necessary to come out on the winning side. Just like any good coach, a good planner has a team of coordinators helping make decisions, including insurance agents, attorneys, accountants, and investment advisors. When the strengths of each of those fields combines, it makes for a winning season and, in financial planning, winning lives.

There are some important questions to ask any advisor with whom you're considering working. Are they capable of looking at the big picture? Firms should be able to offer expertise on each element of a financial plan, whether it be insurance, wealth management, or legal issues. When those elements don't work together, the plan is destined to fail.

How is the planner paid? Are you going to be paying a fee for the plan? Is it an hourly fee, or are commissions involved? If a planner is providing you a "free" plan, chances are he or she may be trying to direct you to a particular kind of investment tied to a commission he will pocket. Other planners, including myself, will charge for the plan based on the client's income. Typically, the higher the income, the more complex the plan can be. At that point, the plan is yours, and it can be implemented however you choose, whether that's on your own, through another firm, or through the firm that produced the plan. This approach eliminates a client feeling obligated to buy a product from someone from whom they received a "free" plan.

What credentials should a financial planner have? Surprisingly, it's scary how little you have to do to call yourself a "financial planner" or "advisor." All it takes is a background check and passing a couple of exams, and you can be in business. Unfortunately, this happens frequently and results in many unqualified people calling themselves a "planner." To become a CERTIFIED FINANCIAL PLANNER™, as I am, requires obtaining the appropriate education and insurance, passing a comprehensive two-day exam, ongoing continuing education, and a set amount of work experience.

If the advisor is someone you'll be trusting for investments, check his or her work and compliance history online (at www.brockercheck.finra.org) to see what licenses he or she holds. You must have a Series 65 or a 66 license to manage money on a fee-only basis, meaning you do not charge commissions to manage money. Advisors with only a Series 6 or 63 license will have to steer you into investments that charge you commission because they can't offer investment advice on a fee-only basis. You're going to be paying for their services based on the commission they charge. There is nothing wrong with commissions, but it's better to work with someone who has the ability to charge on a fee-only basis as well. A simple search on the site also will show if the person has any problems in his or her past as far as complaints, unresolved issues, and whether he or she has been in trouble with the regulatory authorities.

Finally, look at the planner's experience. How long has he or she been in business? Can you see example plans that he or she has done? What other fields has he or she worked in? It can be a red flag if a planner has hopped around a lot or has a reputation for jumping from firm to firm. The planner either may have personal issues or may just be working for the next bigger paycheck.

Certified Public Accountants, or CPAs, are certified in accounting but not investments and financial planning. They are very good at what they do, especially when it comes to preparing financial statements and taxes, but they don't necessarily know everything they need to in order to be a financial planner looking holistically at a person's financial life.

A Chartered Financial Advisor, or CFA, works on choosing stocks and other investments, but typically doesn't provide comprehensive planning services. Our firm has in-house CFAs who help determine, along with other analysts they follow, what stocks, bonds, and other investments are good fits for our clients. They go through a rigorous training and testing regimen to ensure they are the best in their field on analyzing companies, analyzing investments, and making recommendations to advisors and clients. Still, they are not financial planners.

A Chartered Financial Consultant, or ChFC®, is similar to a CFP® but has roots more in the insurance industry. Beyond that, there are many other designations, some legit, but many are the product of someone selling a training course and making a buck. All it takes is someone to put a promise on the Internet saying, "If you pay for my coursework and exams, you can call yourself X, Y, or Z." Watch out for these, especially if it's the only designation your so-called planner has.

With today's technology, the people you choose to work with don't have to be in your backyard. Don't limit yourself to only local professionals. I work with people every day across the United States via phone and Skype. The key is having one-to-one interaction, whether it be in person or in voice alone. Ideally, it's in person, but that's not always realistic. While it may be ideal to work with someone from your local area, it's more important for you to be confident and comfortable with his or her qualifications and he or she as a professional.

Working with people outside your hometown also can provide greater comfort regarding privacy. If you are a farmer in the middle of Arkansas, your local town may or may not have a financial professional capable of handling your particular situation. You may have to look farther away than just the four corners of your county to the person who best suits your needs. I live in an agricultural community of small towns. You wouldn't necessarily recognize the people of means walking down the street, but they're literally the millionaires next door. While those people might trust their financial advisors, they don't necessarily want the people that they interact with socially to know their business.

Many times, these people seek advisors in other cities to ensure word will not travel back to the locale. From a professional standpoint, information is never to be shared with other people. That doesn't necessarily mean it never is. If the person in your hometown does not understand that from a social-interaction standpoint, you may well want to work with someone outside of your geographic area.

There are many financial planners who are truly in the business to work out a plan for your benefit, not theirs. Find one today, and start the process. It will be a lot of work, but you owe it to you and your family. If you take only one thing from this book, let it be this: the comprehensive financial plan is absolutely critical to you and your family's success.

Rule Two

KNOW AND DIRECT YOUR DOLLARS: ACCOUNT, ANALYZE, AND ADJUST

"It's better to look ahead and prepare than to look back and regret."

—JACKIE JOYNER-KERSEE, AMERICAN TRACK-AND-FIELD ATHLETE

When my wife Linda and I were first starting out, we were clueless about personal finance. Both of us were making more money than we ever had before. Fortunately, we were both responsible. Linda grew up with meager means. I had a more comfortable upbringing but was by no means wealthy. We were living in Texas at the time, though "home" was Indiana, so if we found ourselves in a bind, there was no one close to bail us out.

Largely due to fear, we were extremely careful about what we did. Driven by my own personal interest in the subject, I wanted to get a grip on finances very early on in our marriage. I soon discovered Linda and I had two different mind-sets when it came to managing funds. I wanted to account for every penny, nickel, and dime. She saw this as my attempt to control what she spent. I saw it as a way to understand how we spent our money and to help us allocate better. Once we both understood where each was coming from, we began to better understand how to work together to accomplish the goals we had made together as a family. The lesson to be gained from our experience is an important one: If you are a couple, you have to be on the same page. Part of the journey to financial freedom is more than just adding and subtracting—it's about relationships and the psychology of money.

Putting together a comprehensive plan forces you to go through this process together, ensuring your philosophies are in sync. Even if you have a different philosophy than your spouse, your ideas should work together, not against each other. The number-one reason marriages break up is money. Many times, the problems stem from the differing perspectives that each member of the couple brings into the marriage. It's important to realize that the world doesn't revolve around one person. Financial reality revolves around both people, and it begins with creating a budget everyone can adhere to.

TALK IT OUT

Cash-flow planning or "budgeting" is all about accounting, analyzing, and adjusting, and it begins with tracking costs and allocating your income. Adjusting those allocations is a constant process. I recommend reviewing your budget on a monthly basis. Go out to eat, and bring all your financial information with you. Talk about what's coming up in the next month and what you have to look forward to. Ask each other: How does the emergency fund look? What major expenses are we looking at? Are the premiums on the cars due? Do we have money set aside for those things? It's a communication process.

For some, these conversations might be no big deal. For others, they might initially prove difficult but will get easier as time goes on. At least in the beginning, having these talks when dining out makes it as relaxing as possible. Plus, if you do it in a public place, you might be less likely to argue.

It helps if all parties think of budgeting as creating a

road map. A map tells the story of our surroundings, our environment, and even our history. I loved maps when I was a kid because I could imagine visiting places just by looking at them. My first career was in land surveying, which entailed collecting data to make maps or drawings of specific areas. While I'm no longer a surveyor, I still love maps and now collect them, as well as atlases. Even though our smartphones have largely replaced maps for directions, I still like to look at maps to get an overall view, especially when I'm traveling to a new area. Whether we use a map or a GPS to guide us, we must begin with two pieces of information: our current location and our final destination. There might be many different routes to the final destination, but you only have one starting point.

When it comes to your money, you need to know where you are now. Knowing what you spend and where you spend it gives you a starting point. Once you know this, you can start to make adjustments, but until you do, you're just guessing. Without tracking expenses and knowing where every dollar goes, we spend unconsciously and, ultimately, overspend. Not knowing where all your money goes coupled with failure to direct it to where it should will result in fear, anxiety, and blaming each other when the inevitable money crisis hits.

There are many tools to help you track your money. I prefer

Quicken because it's very thorough if you make the effort to include all your accounts. Quicken now has a version you can operate from your smartphone that makes it easy to see clearly in nearly real time where everything is going. Mint is another tool and is completely Internet-based. Whatever tool you prefer, the most important thing is to start using it and to be consistent. Lay everything out on paper or in a spreadsheet, like the one available at RulesToRiches.com, and get started.

The more information you can provide and the more truthful and realistic you can be, the better. Without a clear picture, we live with the constant temptation to spend all the money in our wallets simply because it's there. Credit cards are even worse. We tend to overuse credit cards because there is seemingly no end to their spending power. It takes discipline and mindfulness to think through your spending. Without a plan in place, you'll give little thought to spending that next dollar for a cup of coffee at Starbucks or to walking out the door in the morning without a packed lunch. But if you're mindful, you'll have a plan to protect you from such distractions.

As previously mentioned, spouses must be involved in creating a budget, and at first, you might be surprised to see how money is spent. Take your time, air it out, and take heart. It will become easier as time goes on. The reality is sometimes harder to face, but if you're committed to financial freedom, this is an absolutely necessary step. Information is power, and once you know where all your money goes, you can better plan for your future and achieve your goals. Taking the time to do this early in a marriage or even before a marriage means less strife in the future. Money is one of those subjects you simply must talk about.

MAKE IT HAPPEN

While a financial planner can make a plan for you, only you can make it a reality. If the plan sits in a binder on the shelf, it's useless. You have to implement the plan and work at it consistently. Financial planners can help, but they're not going to be the ones going to dinner with you every month to plan for what's ahead.

When it comes to tracking expenses, think far beyond the big-ticket items. You need to track everything. Initially, you need to save receipts, especially those cash purchases that tend to get by us: the lunches, the coffees, the gifts. Food-related spending tends to be surprising once we start adding it all up. We don't think we give a lot of gifts, but by the time you add up cards, gift cards, and tokens of appreciation we purchase throughout the year, the costs can be significant. In your plan, create a gift budget, and understand how much you're spending and when.

Estimates and actual spending are almost always different. When I do financial plans for people, it's common that 10 to 15 percent of their income initially goes unaccounted for. Grabbing pen and paper and physically writing down what comes in and what goes out is the best way to start.

The Family Budget Planner provides an example of an effective budgeting worksheet (available at RulesToRiches. com). This gives you a full year's view. If you only pay for your car insurance twice a year, you can see exactly when that money is spent and what kind of an impact it has on cash flow. Be sure to customize your own plan to fit your needs. For instance, not everyone needs a line for child care. Use your judgment as to what best serves you.

Yearly Budget Calculator

Note that this calculator appears courtesy of Vertex42.com and is abbreviated for the purposes of space. The full budget calculator can be found at www.vertex42.com/Calculators/budget-calculator.html

A Percentage Guideline also provides recommendations for where to direct your spending and how much of your income you should spend in each category. A disclaimer: I take a very conservative approach and realize some of these guidelines will be tough to meet in areas where housing prices are extremely high. But spending excessively on housing is one of the top reasons why people don't reach their financial goals. I recommend concentrating no more than 20 to 23 percent of your income on housing. Banks and real estate agents will disagree. They would love to see you spending between 30 and 36 percent of your income on housing to include mortgage interest and taxes. This is why so many people find themselves house poor, working full-time just to eke out the mortgage every month and not having anything left over. Be mindful of that before you sign on the dotted line.

Percentage Guideline for Family Income/Expenses

Gross Income	$25,000	$50,000	$75,000	$100,000	$150,000	$200,000	$250,000	$300,000
Taxes*	14%	20%	22%	25%	25%	25%	25%	25%
Charitable Contributions	10%	10%	10%	10%	10%	11%	11%	11%
Savings/Investments	5-20%	5-20%	5-20%	5-20%	5-20%	5-20%	5-20%	5-20%
Housing**	18-23%	15-20%	15-20%	15-20%	15-20%	15-20%	15-20%	15-20%
Transportation	8-10%	8-10%	8-10%	5-7%	5-7%	5-7%	5-7%	5-7%
Food and Beverage	8-12%	6-10%	5-9%	5-9%	5-9%	5-9%	5-9%	5-9%
Clothing	3-5%	3-5%	2-4%	2-4%	2-4%	2-4%	2-4%	2-4%
Furnishings	2-4%	2-4%	2-4%	1-2%	1-2%	1-2%	1-2%	1-2%
Personal Care & Cash	5-7%	3-5%	2-4%	2-4%	2-4%	2-4%	2-4%	2-4%
Medical & Dental	4-6%	3-5%	3-5%	3-5%	3-5%	3-5%	3-5%	3-5%
Insurance	3-5%	6-8%	7-9%	10-12%	10-12%	10-12%	10-12%	10-12%
Education/Self Improvement	2-3%	1-2%	1-2%	1-2%	1-2%	1-2%	1-2%	1-2%
Installment Payments	4-5%	3-4%	2-3%	0%	0%	0%	0%	0%
Entertainment, Dining, Gifts	1-3%	1-3%	2-4%	3-5%	3-5%	3-5%	3-5%	3-5%
Vacations & Holidays	2-4%	2-4%	2-4%	3-5%	3-5%	2-4%	2-4%	2-4%
Miscellaneous	2-3%	1-2%	1-2%	1-2%	1-2%	1-2%	1-2%	1-2%

*Actual percentage will depend on local, state and federal rates.

**I realize the housing cost guideline appears low but remember from chapter 5 that housing costs can have an extreme impact on achieving your overall financial goals. Housing costs are extremely dependent on the region in which you live and keep in mind this is a zero sum game, if one category increases, you must decrease in another.

I recommend allocating 5–10 percent of your income for groceries and another 1–5 percent for eating out and entertainment. Business lunches are fine, depending on the reimbursement policy where you work, but casual meals and coffees can become real sinkholes. All of these ranges are guidelines, not strict rules, but if you do adhere to them, you'll be in a much better financial position than you would otherwise. You will be mindful of what you spend, and that's half the battle.

There are some sieves money passes through that can throw things off track. One of them is emergencies. The transmission breaks on the car, but you have to get to work. If that's not planned for, it puts a strain on your finances. Cash purchases such as eating out, Starbucks, and gifts are expenses that add up very quickly. I prefer to give myself a cash allowance and use it to make those minor purchases. Once that cash is gone, it's gone until I replenish it when I get my next paycheck. That allowance gives me some flexibility while still keeping my plan intact.

When recording what you spend, be scrupulous. Oftentimes, what you think you spend is different than what you really spend. Until you get into the habit of actually recording every expense, you have no idea where your money goes. In this day and age, most of our expenses are recorded, either through our debit-card statements or checking-account withdrawals. It's just a matter of getting them organized so you can understand where your money really is going.

Remember the budgeting exercise we started with? We established that your inflows minus outflows should equal zero. All the money needs to be accounted for, and you can't go into the negative, so when you take money from one area of spending, you have to make it up from another. Think of it as moving money from one bucket to another. This process is a constant and dynamic process, and making such adjustments requires communication with your partner.

If, during one of your monthly reviews, you see a surplus, it's time to discuss where to put it, whether that be toward your savings goal, vehicle replacement, emergency fund, vacation, or gifts budget. If you went in the hole and had to use the credit card, discuss how you will make adjustments accordingly to make sure that doesn't happen going forward. The bottom line: Make sure your yearnings don't exceed your earnings.

Automatic payments can allow you to plan better. Having the electricity bill, water bill, garbage bill, savings, and mortgage removed regularly from your bank account every month helps you manage those payments and makes sure you're never late. You still have to monitor your usage and be mindful you're not overusing utilities, but it can help immensely with record keeping.

All of this will make you become more aware of what you spend. Many of us go through life spending unconsciously because it seems to have worked for us this long. We've managed, at least in our own minds, to stay ahead of the game. But when your financial plan forces you to dig deep, you come to the realization you are not as in control as you thought. You become conscious of your situation, and that allows you to make a plan and spend accordingly.

3

Rule Three

BE A SQUIRREL: HAVE A SAVINGS OR EMERGENCY FUND

"Someone's sitting in the shade today because someone planted a tree a long time ago."

—WARREN BUFFETT, BUSINESSMAN, INVESTOR, AND PHILANTHROPIST

There are many squirrels living around my home in northern Indiana, where winters are notoriously harsh. For a long time, I wondered how these creatures were able to make it through the unforgiving season. I learned the answer simply by watching them. Squirrels seem to be always busy. They play, they fight, but most of the time they're either looking for or consuming food. Squirrels are industrious and ingenious when it comes to food. They don't just eat one thing—they eat hickory nuts, acorns, sunflower seeds, and corn. They have a well-rounded list of many options. They diversify their risk. They adapt to a changing environment. In this way, squirrels can teach us more about money than most people can.

We don't grow sunflowers where I live, yet the squirrels are adept at stealing sunflower seeds from the bird feeder. How do they even know what a sunflower seed is? They tried something different. Whereas humans are creatures of habit, squirrels have no problem working outside the box. They also exhibit great common sense, as evident by their tendency to store food for times when they know it won't be readily available. How many humans are that disciplined when it comes to saving money for use in an emergency? According to statistics, not many.

Almost one-third of Americans have absolutely no savings specifically designated to handle emergencies. It's little wonder why the average person who carries a credit card has a balance over $15,000. The average homeowner who has a mortgage has over $160,000 in debt. Each household that has outstanding car loans has an average balance of $27,000. Student loans average around $47,000. It's clear people are spending what they don't have, which makes establishing an emergency fund even more critical.

Having money "squirreled" away for when things go wrong allows us to have some peace of mind in times of financial trials. We've anticipated the unknown emergency and taken care of it before the long-lasting impact of additional debt can emerge. We anticipate what we can because we know it's not "if" but "when" an emergency will arise.

Despite all evidence to the contrary, most people tell themselves, "It will never happen to me." These are the same people who rely on credit cards to pay for a new transmission or to repair the air conditioning or refrigerator when those things inevitably break. But credit is not real money—it's somebody else's money. Relying on it only lands you deeper in debt. Without an emergency fund, you risk losing your home or property and being forced to declare bankruptcy. We know financial issues are one of the leading causes of stress, which can impact everything from your health to your relationships. Finances affect far more than just our pocketbooks.

GET READY FOR WINTER

A squirrel doesn't just put away food for one winter season. He puts it away for every winter season. Humans are not as disciplined as squirrels in this regard. Granted, the squirrel doesn't have as many distractions from savings as humans do. The squirrel doesn't have advertisements flashing in front of him every day and night, showing him things he doesn't need but making him want them nonetheless. We have to overcome such temptations to become more squirrel-like and start saving for the inevitable winter season.

If you have no savings, get started by putting away $1,000 for a short-term Band-Aid. That $1,000 might seem insurmountable, but your savings can add up very quickly if you're dedicated to the goal. Start small, and build it up. Hold a garage sale. Pick up a part-time job. Do anything you can in any small way, shape, or form to scrape together $1,000.

For the majority of people, $1,000 is not enough to account for all emergencies. Long-term, I suggest saving three to six months' worth of living expenses. Living expenses are defined as food, shelter, clothing, and transportation. They do not include savings or making payments on unsecured debt. Living expenses are the things that keep our families safe, warm, fed, and clothed. For instance, shelter includes utilities, but it does not include cable TV. Clothing includes shoes and pants and socks, but it does not include going to Macy's to buy things new. It might include going to the Goodwill store. Remember, when saving this money, you are anticipating a catastrophic event such as the loss of a job or a short-term disability. In this scenario, you don't have any money coming in, and you are in survival mode.

The amount you will save for this fund likely will be far less than what you typically spend in a three- or six-month span. For example, if your monthly budget is $5,000, but that includes cable TV, Internet, dry cleaning, and new clothes, you can cut all of those things out when anticipating an emergency.

In a long-term emergency, payments on unsecured debt such as credit cards, department store debt, and furniture loans must be set aside. If you don't have the money, temporarily pause your payments. It's important to communicate with your creditors and explain your situation, but don't expect them to be sympathetic or immediately offer alternatives. They might hound you, but do not pay them a dime if you need the money for the critical elements of survival. After you miss several payments, they might be more accommodating and work with you to lower your minimum payments or interest rates. Whatever they offer you, always get any promise from a creditor in writing and follow up with your part of the bargain. If you told them you're going to send them twenty dollars, then by all means, send them twenty dollars. They like to see a record of following through with payment, which shows responsibility. Once you're through the valley of the crisis, start an accelerated payment plan. Get out of the debt, and destroy your credit cards.

Some people will worry this will ruin their credit scores. It might, but don't sacrifice your family's well-being for a credit score. If you don't have money and you can't pay your debts, your credit score doesn't mean much anyway. It should be the least of your concerns when coping with a true emergency.

STASH YOUR STOCKPILE

Once you have your emergency fund, do not keep it in your checking account. Use a totally different bank away from where you regularly do business to avoid the temptation to tap into it. Even if you leave it as a cushion in your checking account, you'll always know that money is there. Put it somewhere where it's inconvenient to access yet still obtainable. It helps if getting to it requires a little extra effort.

When an emergency happens, the first thing you must determine is whether it is a one-time unexpected large expense or something requiring more long-term attention. If a car breaks in the dead of winter, it's a one-time incident, and you should feel comfortable using the emergency fund. If it's something resulting in a money shortfall for an extended period of time, you may need to make more fundamental changes to your budget, and you need to do so quickly. Still, in this same scenario, you may also need to accommodate one-time extraordinary expenses. For example, if new clothes become a priority for a job interview, you may have to make adjustments to free up more money. If your housing situation is such that you can save money by moving to another house, it might be time to move. Your goal is to keep the four walls of survival intact. It's acceptable to make adjustments for things that will help get you out of the hole.

The overriding consideration has to be the question, "What do I have to do to keep my family taken care of?" Question every expenditure. Ask, "Is this critical to keeping my family fed, sheltered, clothed, or transported to work, school, or the doctor?" Scrutinize what you spend, and be cautious of making any unnecessary purchases until the emergency has passed.

Rule Four

SAVE, THEN PAY

"Too many people spend money they haven't earned to buy things they don't want to impress people they don't like."

—WILL ROGERS, PERFORMER AND
SOCIAL COMMENTATOR

When it comes to obtaining financial freedom, history has much to teach us. Before World War II, most people dealt exclusively with cash, as credit carried a certain stigma. If you used credit, many people assumed you were not a good money manager. It suggested you had personal problems that led to financial distress. Instead of credit cards, retailers offered layaway plans. You would shop at a department or furniture store and choose the items you liked. You would put money down on them, but you wouldn't walk out of the store with them. They stayed there until you came back and made payments toward the bill. Once it was paid for, only then did you take it home. It was the ideal solution when people couldn't afford a big purchase.

It also was a harbinger for things to come. With new media sources such as radio and television, the power of advertising and marketing was quickly making its presence felt in the lives of Middle America. Credit emerged as a solution to the problem of mismatched cash flows. The grocery stores extended credit to families, not necessarily because they couldn't pay, but because they only got paid once a month. As long as they were consistent on paying the grocers back, there was no problem. There were no traditional credit cards. After World War II, all the returning veterans needed new homes and furniture to fill them with, thus leading to the country's first wave of debt financing. Home mortgages became prevalent, furniture was financed on store charge cards, and layaway became less prevalent thanks to easy credit. Back then, there was no MasterCard or Visa. If you wanted to buy something on credit at a department store such as Sears or J. C. Penney's, you had to go through their own credit departments. Credit cards didn't really exist on their own until 1950 when Diner's Club was created, and American Express, Visa, and MasterCard followed.

After the war, Americans also started our love affair with the automobile. Automakers became more mindful in their marketing efforts, and everyone wanted one. As automobiles were the most expensive thing people bought after their homes, manufacturers extended credit for purchasing vehicles. Today, very few people buy a car without taking out a loan, and more often than not, the vehicle they choose is far more extravagant than what they truly need. We see commercials and are promised we can make easy payments and extend payments for several years. Some offer up to eighty-four months to pay off a car, though some vehicles will not even stay in working order that long. Over the last decade, leasing also has become popular. While leasing is a way to drive a new car with typically lower payments, you own nothing at the end of the agreement. You're left with the option of either leasing another car, potentially paying a penalty for exceeding allowed mileage, purchasing outright the car you leased, or having to purchase another vehicle. Unlike home leases, you are obligated to carry insurance on the physical car itself and maintain the car to a set of required standards.

"Low" monthly payments created by lengthening credit terms and cheap leases are just one way marketing has made our wants seem like needs, and easy access to credit has legitimized our spending. Credit-card debt in this country now exceeds a trillion dollars. Auto loans also exceed a trillion dollars. Credit has accelerated our spending and the idea of saving for something before you pay for it is a novelty. It shouldn't be.

ASSESS AND ANTICIPATE

As part of your financial plan, you should think critically about your future needs. Set aside a portion of your income every month to address the need, and keep track of it in one of the many available financial apps or a spreadsheet like the Savings Goal Tracker referenced in chapter 1. This allows you to look ahead to your future needs and save for each one. Think of it as a reverse loan. You end up being your own bank, earning interest instead of paying interest.

Home repairs are a constant burden. Any of a number of things can and will go wrong, whether it is a roof in need of replacement, a broken air conditioner, or a burst pipe. Vehicle replacement is another priority. You might not buy a new car, but the car you currently have will at some point need to be replaced. Instead of taking a loan, save now in anticipation of that day. Maintaining the emergency fund always is important. Other areas for saving include vacations, Christmas gifts, and starting a business—and the list can go on and on. Regardless of what your specific goals are, the list should be fashioned based on the things you know you can anticipate spending money on in the future.

Use the sinking fund concept when it comes to large planned expenditures. If one of your goals is to start a business, realize it's not just a matter of quitting a job one day and launching your new business the next. You have to plan for the initial expenses. One of the main causes for failure of a new business is lack of sufficient capital at the onset. By nature, things move slowly in the beginning, and you'll need capital to get over that hump. Anticipate what equipment, inventory, and labor you will need. If you'll be quitting your job to start the business, consider your living expenses. If it's a franchise, find out what you're going to have to pay to start that business. (See chapter 7 to learn more about the financial and personal advantages of starting a business.)

While you can keep funds designated for larger future expenses at the same bank where you regularly do business, I suggest moving them to a separate savings account. Make it slightly easier to access than your emergency fund, and set it up so you can transfer funds from the account to your checking account. Tying a debit card to the account only adds to the temptation to spend it. Instead, make transfers to your checking account as expenses arise. Overall, you will have the following accounts:

1. A checking account tied to a debit card, which will pay for everyday living expenses.
2. An emergency fund in a savings account at a different bank from the one where your regular checking account is located.
3. Your savings accumulation fund, either at the same bank where your checking account is located or at another bank where funds can easily be transferred in and out.

There are other specific kinds of savings accounts available, depending on each family's needs. Many need a college savings account. Tax-advantaged options such as a 529 plan allow you to save money for education while avoiding tax on the gain, provided the money is used for college expenses upon withdrawal. In some states, contributions to a 529 plan provide a state income-tax credit. Failing to take advantage of such an account when you know you'll have college expenses in the future is like leaving money on the table. A Coverdell account is another tax-advantaged plan that allows you to pay for private primary and secondary school as well as college. Once people reach age forty, retirement savings becomes a huge priority. Many times, they come to the realization that they haven't saved as much as they should have. There are several different tax-advantaged plans that can help them reach their goals, including 401(k)s, IRAs, 457 plans, 403(b) plans, Roth IRAs, and Roth 401(k)s. All of these allow you to either defer or avoid taxes altogether. See chapter 6 for more in-depth information on investing and saving for retirement.

When it comes to the question of how much to save, everyone's needs are different. There are so many moving pieces that no generalized answer exists. It depends on your specific situation, all your assets and liabilities, and your goals and aspirations. Conducting a comprehensive overview of your financial health will help you see what you'll need to adequately fund your future.

DO YOUR HOMEWORK

While everyone's financial outlook is different, many share one common burden: student loans. Paying for college has become more of an expectation than an option for today's parents. Whether we like it or not, those who don't take on the full responsibility of funding their child's education can be labeled by some as somehow inadequate. Fear of such labels often causes parents to unwisely divert money from their retirement savings to their child's education.

I believe paying for a child's entire education can actually be harmful. The child learns little about accountability and risks developing a sense of entitlement. Later in life, he or she will expect the same treatment when it's time to buy a new car or even a house. Furthermore, if the parents don't save enough for retirement, the child could end up supporting them. I recommend that parents and children share the costs of education, and both should be saving long before it's time to enroll. Opening one of the aforementioned tax-advantaged savings accounts is a great way to start.

Our kids paid for half of their college expenditures and earned college credit at community college before advancing to their state schools of choice. Attending an affordable community college to determine what major fits you best is an ideal alternative to spending a small fortune for the first two years at a private or state school and discovering you're unhappy with your choice. From my own personal experience in the corporate world, I can attest that few employers care about where candidates attend college as long as the school is accredited and reputable. Personal qualities such as work ethic, timeliness, and responsibility are far more valued in today's working world. There is no harm in spreading a college career over two different schools, provided it makes the most economic sense.

Also, when considering sources of funding, don't overlook the benefit of scholarships. There is an abundance of free money available, and it's not reserved for kids in the top 10 percent of their class. My wife is a high school teacher. Every year, her school holds an awards day. It's amazing how many kids are awarded tens of thousands of dollars from companies all over the country. For instance, Burger King awards a substantial scholarship to one of our students nearly every year. The student does not even have to work at Burger King, but rather has to be actively involved in community service. Eli Lilly, a pharmaceutical company based in Indianapolis, pays full tuition to any state school for hundreds of kids across our state based on merit, community involvement, and need. If you look good on paper, there is money to be had. Completing the applications can be demanding on both your time and energy, but look at it as honing a skill. Life often requires us to present ourselves to others and communicate our special skills, which doesn't come easy for most of us. The more you practice, the better you become.

GET BACK IN THE BLACK

Debt is the most destructive factor holding us back from achieving our financial goals, and every comprehensive financial plan must include a strategy for eliminating it. The Debt Reduction Calculator (found at RulesToRiches. com) shows you how to supercharge your debt-reduction plan so you eliminate all debt quicker than most anyone can imagine. This is an amazing tool—I see people sit stunned in disbelief when I show them that they can be debt-free, including their mortgage, in as little as a few years. Everyone's situation is different, but regardless of your circumstances, what do you have to lose except debt?

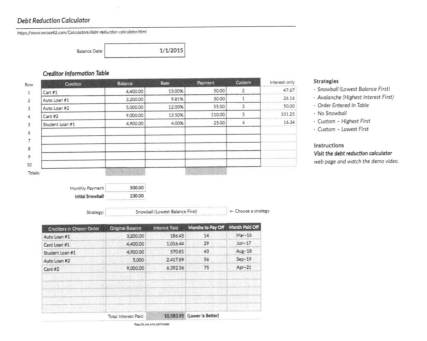

Debt Reduction Calculator

https://www.vertex42.com/Calculators/debt-reduction-calculator.html

Balance Date: 1/1/2015

Creditor Information Table

Row	Creditor	Balance	Rate	Payment	Custom	Interest-only
1	Cart #1	4,400.00	13.00%	50.00	2	47.67
2	Auto Loan #1	3,200.00	9.81%	30.00	1	26.16
3	Auto Loan #2	5,000.00	12.00%	55.00	3	50.00
4	Card #2	9,000.00	13.50%	110.00	5	101.25
5	Student Loan #1	4,900.00	4.00%	25.00	4	16.34
6						
7						
8						
9						
10						
Totals:						

Strategies
· *Snowball (Lowest Balance First)*
· *Avalanche (Highest Interest First)*
· *Order Entered In Table*
· *No Snowball*
· *Custom – Highest First*
· *Custom – Lowest First*

Instructions
Visit the debt reduction calculator web page and watch the demo video.

Monthly Payment: 500.00
Initial Snowball: 230.00

Strategy: Snowball (Lowest Balance First) ← Choose a strategy

Creditors in Chosen Order	Original Balance	Interest Paid	Months to Pay Off	Month Paid Off
Auto Loan #1	3,200.00	186.45	14	Mar-16
Card #1	4,400.00	1,016.44	29	Jun-17
Student Loan #1	4,900.00	570.81	43	Aug-18
Auto Loan #2	5,000	2,417.89	56	Sep-19
Card #2	9,000.00	6,392.36	75	Apr-21

Total Interest Paid: 10,583.95 (Lower Is Better)

Results are only estimates

This calculator appears courtesy of Vertex42 and can be found at https://www.vertex42.com/Calculators/debt-reduction-calculator.html

If you have credit cards, pay them off and never use them again—it's that simple and yet that hard. Otherwise, if you choose to continue using them, you must have the discipline to pay them off every month. Credit cards can offer an easy way to track expenses, and users are tempted by the rewards programs tied to them, but it's crucial to understand that it is not actual physical cash coming in and out of your plan. No one has ever added to their net worth by spending more on their credit card just to get the rewards.

When it comes to cars, save yourself years of financial stress by saving then paying. If you're just starting out, skip the new-car showroom, even if you're making more money than you ever have before. Look for a well-maintained used car, preferably something you can buy outright or with affordable, short-term monthly payments. Or, if you live in a city, skip the car purchase altogether and opt for public transportation.

Never go into debt for a retail purchase. The zero-percent interest rate at your local furniture store might seem tempting, but why not save and pay cash for that couch? I can guarantee that if you walk into the store and offer to pay cash, the price will magically drop.

The purchase of a home is truly the only thing one should ever consider financing. If you're saving then paying, there is little else for which you should go into debt. If you do have to finance a home, consider paying a larger down payment and securing a loan for less than thirty years.

By doing both, you will be out of debt sooner, which is always the goal.

Rule Five

CURB YOUR ENTHUSIASM

"The size of one's house might bear a relationship to the size of one's opinion of oneself, but it has nothing to do with one's real worth."

—ALEXANDER MCCALL SMITH, AUTHOR AND CREATOR OF *THE NO. 1 LADIES' DETECTIVE AGENCY* NOVEL SERIES

In order to see where the bulk of the average person's income is spent, one need look no farther than the curb. The curb you live on and what you park on that curb requires the vast majority of your money. For many of us, our homes and cars also often cost more than we realistically can afford. While there is nothing wrong with having a nice home or car, few of us can truly afford them.

Allow me to describe a scenario that might ring true: You, a couple in your early thirties who both have jobs outside the home, buy a small starter home. It's nice at first, but it very quickly becomes too small for your growing family. It's close to work, but you long for one of those bigger homes in the suburbs. You decide to look for a bigger home, even if it means a longer commute. The first thing the realtor asks is, "What's your income?" By asking this, the realtor is determining the size of the loan for which you will qualify.

Mortgage underwriter criteria say you can spend up to 36 percent of your income on housing. If you and your spouse make a combined $150,000, that means, according to the mortgage lenders, you can afford a $700,000 house.

You get excited and immediately start looking online. Before you know it, you find your dream home, and it's $800,000. The mortgage company qualifies you for a $750,000 loan. They don't care if you're on track with retirement savings or college savings or emergency fund savings. They care about income and debt ratios. On paper, they say you can afford the house.

Before the closing, you look into homeowner's insurance. It's more than you pay now, but you assume you'll be generating more income the longer you work. You look at property taxes and utilities. They too are more than you pay now, but again, you're going to be making more, so it's fine.

You close on the house, and you're ecstatic! But it soon becomes clear you don't have enough furniture to fill it. Knowing furniture stores love to sell their merchandise on credit, you buy $20,000 worth. You tell yourself this is fine, because you will pay it back over time.

You also have a three-car garage and only two cars. Filling the extra space with a boat makes perfect sense.

When you add up all the costs, the house costs you more than $900,000. Both of you now have to work the rest of your lives because you had to have the bigger and better thing. Somewhere along the road, life inevitably will happen. One of you will lose a job, get sick, or become disabled. Now, you don't have enough income to make your payments. You try to sell the house, but the market for an older home with dated styling, technology, location, and demographics is limited at best. Your financial life goes south, and everything is affected: your marriage, your health, your children.

It's a scenario that plays out far too frequently, yet all this suffering could be avoided if society stopped constantly convincing us we need things we don't.

NEEDS VERSUS WANTS

When deciding how to spend your income, consider the difference between needs and wants. A need is something you must have to survive; a want is not. This seems straightforward, but for many of us, it becomes increasingly blurry the second we set foot in the grocery store, visit Amazon, go to the car dealer, or talk to a realtor.

In reality, our needs are limited to four basic things to survive: shelter, food, clothing, and basic transportation. Shelter can be a four-bedroom, three-bath, three-car-garage house, or it can be a zero-bedroom, one-bath, zero-car-garage efficiency apartment. Both are shelter. You also need food and water. You can drink tap water the same way you can drink Fiji bottled water. Chicken feeds you just as well as steak. Your clothing can come from Goodwill, or it can come from Neiman Marcus. Transportation can be satisfied with a paid-for ten-year-old Toyota Corolla or a brand-new Lexus with zero money down and "easy" payments for eighty-four months. Every one of these options meets a need, but some go beyond the basics to become "wants." I'm not implying you should only buy the things that meet the basic needs. Life is meant to be enjoyed. Pick and choose where you will splurge on the "wants." Treat yourself reasonably—but only when you can afford it.

So many of us spend our lives accumulating "stuff." I go

to estate auctions often, and while I occasionally find a great bargain, the events themselves are very depressing. The sellers are usually hawking the former belongings of their deceased loved ones. As we know, you can't take it with you, so instead, it's left to the loved ones to sell it all to strangers. It could all be avoided if more of us put the same importance on relationships we typically reserve for "stuff." Your enduring legacy lives through people. Strive for meaningful relationships, and make a difference in those people's lives. Look critically at what you value, and surround yourself only with the things necessary to feed those values.

There is a verse in the Gospel of Mark that says, "What shall it profit a man if he shall gain the whole world and lose his own soul?" (Mark 8:36). It is a terrifying analogy between spiritual profit and worldly profit. It urges us to ask, "At the end of this life, what really matters: the stuff we have or the relationships we've cultivated throughout our lifetimes?" Will people remember and value the positive influence you had on their lives or that you gave them a great sweater one year for Christmas? Will they remember how you helped shape their outlook, or will they remember what car you drove? Without a doubt, the positive influence you had on their lives will be more lasting and meaningful. Before any major purchase, I urge you to read these last few paragraphs again. You will never regret letting your true values guide your decisions.

People want things they don't need largely because of advertising, a concept that exists solely to separate you from your money. We must learn how to distance ourselves from the toxicity of advertising. It is capable of overtaking people in many different ways, particularly in America where its influence is incessant. In this country, it's led us to see first-world inconveniences as third-world problems. Consider that at the turn of the last century, humans barely had the luxury of indoor plumbing let alone indoor bathrooms. Now, we stress over the decision whether to buy a two- or three-bathroom home. Much of the world's population still does not have indoor plumbing. Thus, the decision of how many bathrooms to have in your home is a first-world problem masquerading as a third-world problem. We've lost our ability to discern between the two, and it's evolved into an issue of entitlement. We see our next-door neighbor or family members or friends with something new and decide we're worthy of it as well. This dictates how we manage our money and, ultimately, our needs and wants.

Much of society's widespread tendency to make poor financial decisions also can be attributed to lack of parental guidance and education. When children are in school, we spend so much time worrying about their ability to master the basics of every subject. For reasons I've never understood, money management is not one of them. Understanding a credit-card statement, balancing a checkbook, and learning to budget are life skills everyone needs. The act of overlooking their importance borders on negligence. Yet people avoid talking about money. My family never spoke of it, and over time, it became a very guarded, off-limits topic. While people certainly have the right to be private, I have seen situations where this kind of secrecy leads to problems. I've seen parents who never discuss their financial situation with their adult children, and when an illness or death occurs, no one knows what to do. I believe anyone who is creating a comprehensive plan should inform their adult children of their situation. Not everyone loves to hear this. Some fear admitting they are not as successful as what their lifestyle indicates. Others fear people will be "out to get their money." Operating on such fear keeps us from seeing the positive things in life.

As humans, it is our nature to look at what others have and want it for ourselves. At times, this causes us to overlook our "needs" and worry only about our "wants." Allowing those priorities to shift can be dangerous. Books like *Millionaire Next Door* by Thomas J. Stanley and William Danko and Stanley's follow-up *Stop Acting Rich* taught us there are rich people living next to most of us who have very modest lifestyles. They have built up a net worth over many years and have much to show for it, but they don't flaunt their wealth. They buy used cars and modest homes. They give to their churches. They teach the importance of having a solid work ethic to their kids. They help their kids, but they don't buy everything for them. They value education but realize success is much more than a college degree. They are welders, auctioneers, and other blue-collar workers you would never assume are rich. Maybe they're managing a small business that has done very well due largely to its reputation. No matter what they do, they all have saved, and they have something to show for it at the end of their working careers.

DO THE MATH

Regardless of what society would lead you to believe, your house in not an investment. Buying a home is by no means a surefire way to ensure financial security. In fact, in some cases, it can accomplish the exact opposite.

It's important to take all of this into consideration when calculating how much house you really can afford. In my experience, most home-affordability calculators are woefully inadequate. They ask for only three pieces of information: annual income, down payment, and monthly debt. For a family making $100,000 a year with a down payment of $10,000 and monthly debt of $350, one of the online calculators I used says you can buy a house listed at $469,990.

Notice they didn't ask what your household expenses are, whether your kids go to public or private school, whether you're saving 10 percent of your income for retirement, whether you're saving for your child's education, whether you give to church, whether at some point one spouse is considering staying at home to care for the kids, or whether this new, nearly $500,000 house will take thousands of dollars of new furniture to fill it up. Also notice that most of these calculators, when presented online, are sponsored by real-estate firms and lenders, both of which stand to benefit from selling you a bigger, more expensive home.

According to common practice, these calculators assume you can afford to spend 36 percent of your income on housing. I'd argue that figure should be much closer to 25 percent and ideally below. Perhaps that means you're not buying the home of your dreams, but you still can find something well suited for you and your family.

Think about how much space you really need and how long you will be in the house. Is there a possibility, because of work or other circumstances, that you'll be leaving in a few years? Consider the ancillary expenses that will go along with the house, such as new furniture, lawn care, insurance, utilities, maintenance, and repairs. Think about how a move will affect your commute. Think about the quality of schools in the area.

When you ask yourself these questions, you're defining value. It's very tempting to assign value to things that don't matter, such as square footage. When looking at homes in Texas, my wife and I nearly fell for the real-estate listings touting the highest square footage. Fortunately, we were working with a real-estate agent who argued location is far more important than size. If you're in a massive home in a terrible neighborhood, you clearly have not made a good decision. Many times, the square footage of a home becomes secondary to the location.

For younger families, the quality of the school system is often the most important variable. If a school's performance declines over time, you can expect to see property values drop as well. If you're looking in an area where small homes are rather expensive, chances are the school district is very high quality. People are willing to pay more for homes because they don't have to foot the bill for private school. Other variables affecting the value of a home can include access to shopping, parks and recreation, and health care, and a good real-estate agent can provide information on each. We don't say "location, location, location" for no reason.

This might seem like a lot to consider, but your home is most likely the largest expense of your life. Once you sign the papers, you're committed for a very long time to an incredibly large expense. Note that I said "expense," not investment, unless you are planning to be a landlord. If you choose to invest in real estate, make it a part of a long-term wealth-building strategy. Never buy a home or rental property assuming you are going to make money. Between the cost of maintenance and the potential of a down market, it can be risky. I've personally experienced loss due to a down market. I bought a condo in Houston in 1981 for $54,000 and sold it four years later for $17,000. At the time the local market was tied to the price of oil, which is notorious for fluctuating. When I tried to sell, prices were down. I was stuck paying off the rest of the note, which was not fun, needless to say.

We bought a house in 1997 for $151,000 and sold it in 2003 for $180,000. We bought another house in 2003 for $330,000 and sold it in 2005 for $270,000. That same house sold recently for $460,000. This all just shows how fickle real estate can be.

Don't automatically assume buying is the best thing—start

out renting a home in the area you think you want to live and can afford. Depending on that experience, you may be persuaded that buying makes the most economic sense. People unfairly assign a certain stigma to renters. People love to say you're "throwing your money away," when in reality, making a decent return on the purchase of a home is not easy. But misery loves company, and while your friends can go on and on about how wonderful their house is and how much they enjoy it, you know the tremendous cost it requires.

When deciding on a real-estate agent, I recommend asking your potential agent the following fifteen questions, provided by Redfin.com:

1. Is this your full-time gig? How many clients have you served this year? If the person is an active full-time agent, they are more likely to be up-to-date on the market and the law.

2. How many sales have you handled in my target neighborhoods? You want someone who knows the local market with a few recent deals in your target neighborhoods.

3. When clients aren't happy with your service, what has gone wrong? Asking why a client has been a bad fit for an agent can help you figure out if you're a good fit or not.

4. Has a client ever filed a complaint against you? If you're uncomfortable asking that question, just check with your state's licensing board.

5. What is your fee? The seller pays the buyer's agent using the money you pay for the house, typically 2 to 3 percent of the sales price. Because the commission amount is set by the seller, the amount can vary from home to home. Insist that your agent is up-front about his share to avoid working with someone who pressures you into a home based on his chances of landing a fatter commission check.

6. What services do you offer beyond negotiations in escrow? Make a list of what you'll be paying for. Negotiations, paperwork, and contingencies are the minimum.

7. When am I committed to working with you? Many consumers start touring homes without realizing this can obligate them to work with the agent, contract or no contract.

8. How many foreclosure or short-sale transactions have you handled? Distressed properties can be great deals, but the paperwork is complicated, and your liability is greater. The best agents have experience closing deals with banks.

9. Who else will be working with me? An agent is often supported by a team, but the person you hire should do most of the work.

10. Am I obligated to work with the lender, inspector, or other service providers you recommend? A yes here is a big red flag. Though good agents may have solid recommendations for lenders, inspectors, or other service providers, you should never feel pressured to use the recommendations. It's illegal for an agent to force you to use his or her lender or other service provider.

11. How quickly can you get me into a home? Ask how the agent handles tours on short notice.

12. Do you represent buyers and sellers on the same house? When one agent represents both the buyer and seller, it's known as "dual agency," and it's not a good thing for buyers. If the seller's agent is trying to get the most money for his client's home, how can he also be trying to get you the best deal? Avoid dual agencies. You have to make sure the agent has your best interest at heart, and the best way to do so is to go through a buyer's agent.

13. What sets you apart from other agents? Look for expertise, not just enthusiasm. You want an agent with experience in your favorite neighborhoods, a proven track record of happy customers, and deep knowledge of any special requirements you might have in a home search.

14. What if I'm unhappy with your service? Most agents get paid when you buy a home, which gives them an incentive to close the deal regardless of your doubts or complaints. Ask your agent if he or she is willing to guarantee your satisfaction.

15. Can I see reviews of your past deals? Every agent has clients he served well, but the best agents consistently deliver excellent service. There's a difference between reading a few handpicked endorsements and getting the full good, bad, and ugly on your agent. A good agent should have nothing to hide. You can use sites such as Yelp.com to view real customer opinions for an agent you're considering.

THE DRIVING FORCE

In my lifetime, I've wasted so much money on nice cars that I'm scared to calculate the total. Had I taken that money and put it into a mutual fund, I suspect I'd be looking at six figures. I pray it's not closer to seven. Had I been more practical, I would have realized early on that cars are nothing more than transportation. The majority of wealthy people do not buy expensive new cars. They don't trade cars every few years, nor do they lease cars. The majority buy quality used cars and keep them for a long time, often seven or more years. Learn from these millionaires, and if you're thinking about buying a nice new car, stop right now.

Most likely, there is a used vehicle out there that will meet your needs. Buy it, and keep it as long as you can. The key to buying used vehicles is patience. Searching for a good used car can take time and energy. My son recently was looking for a vehicle and knew something used would meet his needs. He was more interested in cost and function than the brand and type. We scoured Craigslist, eBay, Autotrader.com, Cars.com, and KBB.com and were on the lookout every time we drove around town. We never looked at the local dealerships. We soon learned that if you don't need a car within a short amount of time, the cars come to you. His budget was under $5,000. We knew we had to be unafraid of cars with over a hundred thousand miles. There was a time when anything over a hundred thousand miles wasn't road worthy, but times have changed. Cars are made much better than they used to be. Our family has vehicles ranging from 50,000 miles to 240,000 miles, and ranging in age from twenty years to four years. All are currently running, and the one with 240,000 miles is driven daily. My son ended up buying an eight-year-old car with 113,000 miles, and it runs fine.

There are a few precautions to consider. It's ideal if the seller is also the owner who put the most miles on the vehicle. Avoid those who are trying to wholesale cars as a side business, and be very skeptical of anything bought at a car auction. While some people who do this are reputable, others are selling the offcasts from dealers who are not interested in retailing certain trade-ins. If the dealer doesn't want to take the risk of selling a particular trade-in, there is obviously an issue. Exercise caution when considering a car with a rebuilt title. These are cars that have been damaged in an accident then "totaled" by the insurance company. They are then sold by the insurance company to an individual, body shop, or other entity that will rebuild the vehicle to road-worthy status. Some of the people who rebuild these vehicles do good work, and the buyer gets a car that looks great at a great price. Some are only out to make a quick buck, and their vehicles are disasters on wheels. I have bought a car with a rebuilt title, and still my advice is to steer clear of them unless you are guaranteed the entity you're buying from is legitimate.

When my son was searching for a used car, I helped him look at a 2008 SUV with 88,000 miles. It turned out the person selling it was buying cars from an auction or dealer and then reselling them to the public. Upon inspection, I could see why the dealer didn't want the car on their retail lot. Its frame was heavily rusted, it had clearly been repainted, and it had heavy smoke residue. While it was priced significantly under the Kelley Blue Book value, I walked away.

While the Internet allows for almost unlimited availability of purchasing options, keep in mind that out-of-state cars might require additional inspection and shipping costs. Sometimes you can justify the added expense by the lower price, and if you can't go look at the vehicle in person, you can pay for a service to inspect it and send you a report on its condition. Just use common sense, and remember that if it sounds too good to be true, it probably is.

I also live by the adage that the cheapest car you can operate is the one you already own. Unless the car is in catastrophic shape, I will most always repair rather than replace. This goes back to our budgeting skills: If you set aside money in a sinking fund to repair your vehicles, they should last a long time.

There are a few situations when it makes sense to buy new. A new car with a warranty can be essential if you run a business that involves delivering products or services in a prompt and professional manner. Buying new also makes sense if the dealer is a client in the business you operate. Personal preference is another acceptable reason to buy new, as long as you understand that the instant you drive a new car out of the showroom, it loses 20–30 percent of its value.

Leases may seem attractive, but they are only ideal for those who just can't stand to drive an older car and require a new car every couple of years. This isn't a need; it's a want. At the end of every lease, you have nothing to show for your payments. I prefer to buy a reasonably priced used car, keep that car for a long period of time, maintain it, and then trade it in.

Whenever it's time to replace your vehicle, look to your sinking fund. Instead of buying a vehicle and paying for it after the fact, with this fund you save and actually pay for it up-front. If you make a monthly payment to your sinking fund for vehicle replacement, you are armed with cash when the time comes to buy a new car, which puts you in a better negotiating position, especially with a private seller. Once you've used that money, start saving for the next vehicle again. It is the reverse idea of car purchasing than the one we have today, but it will save you money in the long run.

Should you need more convincing, consider this cringe-worthy personal story. Like most young males of my age, I liked nice cars. I had a good job that paid well but little adult direction on what to do with that money. Between the ages of fifteen and twenty-two, I spent $16,200 on cars. Had I instead put that money in a tax-deferred investment account such as a portfolio of growth stocks, I would have just over $900,000 today (based on the long-term return of the stock market). I consider it tragic to think of the nest egg and legacy I lost due to a lack of knowledge and, more so, discipline. What started as $16,200 would have grown, with no additional contributions or exotic invest-ments, to close to $1 million.

It further pains me to think of what would have happened had I left that money in that account for another twenty years from now. The sum could have grown to just over $9,000,000 (again based on the long-term return of the stock market). Time and compound interest make up the magic that can lead to such results.

When it comes to saving money, hindsight truly is 20/20. Saving is crucial to our financial health, yet we are so easily swayed by the desire for immediate gratification. Fortunately, discipline is a skill that can be taught. The concept of saving money should be emphasized primarily at home, at after-school programs, or even in church. We can let our children and grandchildren learn from our example and reinforce that message by talking to them about the importance of creating a stable financial future for themselves. We should be up-front about money. Our kids don't have to know every detail of our checking account, but letting it all remain a mystery can be harmful. Children need situational counseling, not general guidance. Pass on your wisdom to avoid your child's reliving the same mistakes you made.

Rule Six

SAVE AND INVEST WITH A PURPOSE

"It's not how much money you make, but how much money you keep, how hard it works for you, and how many generations you keep it for."

—ROBERT KIYOSAKI, INVESTOR, AUTHOR,
AND MOTIVATIONAL SPEAKER

When it comes to ensuring your own financial security, the most important thing you can do is save. Saving gives us the freedom to do the things we want, whether it's buying a car or TV, paying for a child's education, or retiring. No one approaching retirement has ever said, "I wish I hadn't saved this much. This is simply too much money."

Saving allows us to live the life we desire. Think of it as a form of delayed gratification, and don't let roadblocks such as impulse purchases or poor planning keep you from the reward.

THE LAW OF COMPOUND INTEREST

As proven by my own missed opportunity to reap its benefits, as detailed in chapter 5, compound interest can be to your extreme advantage when you're investing money over a long period of time. The Power of Compounding image gives an example of two different people. Josh contributed $5,000 per year from age twenty-five to thirty-five for a total of $55,000. Jacob didn't start contributing until age thirty-five and contributed $5,000 per year until age sixty-five for a total of $155,000. Assuming an investment return of 8 percent per year, Josh has a balance 35 percent higher than Jacob's with a third of the amount contributed. Josh only invested for ten years, but he ended up with more money than Jacob, who invested much longer.

Power of Compounding

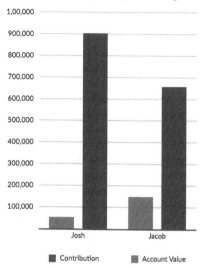

SAVE EARLY

Josh contributed $5,000 per year from age 25 to age 35, for a total of $55,000. Jacob didn't start contributing until age 35 and contributed $5,000 per year until age 65, for a total of $155,000. Assuming an investment return of 8% per year, Josh has a balance more than 35% higher than Jacob's, with a third of the amount contributed.

Starting to invest early is extremely important. The return continues to climb the longer your money stays invested. Once you start, increase the amount you contribute to your investments as your earnings rise. At the end of a forty-year career, you'll have a substantial amount you never would have saved otherwise.

While starting early is key, it's really never too late to start. Some people feel dejected when they look at their investment account or 401(k) statement and realize they don't have enough money to retire. They may have to work longer than they planned or get a second job. Don't dwell on the mistakes you made in the past but learn from them. If your past includes poor money management, make sure it's not part of your future.

SAVE YOURSELF

Consult your comprehensive plan, consider what you are saving for, and allow your goals to guide you to the appropriate investments. Even if you believe you've let too much time pass without saving, start small and contribute whatever you can, whenever you can. Everyone, regardless of income level, needs to save. Savings provides peace of mind, which to many is the most important goal of creating a comprehensive plan. With savings, we know we will be taken care of for a long time, and more importantly, we'll also be taking care of our families. Savings can be used both for emergencies and for long-term needs, as outlined in chapters 3 and 4.

People struggle with saving, also known as delaying gratification, largely because of the constant stream of marketing surrounding us at all times. Online shopping lets us see something we want and get it with a click of a button. Rarely are these purchases things we need, but we want them and we want them now. Spending money used to require a much bigger ordeal. Now it's extremely easy to spend money, particularly money you don't have.

Diminishing work ethic also makes it harder for many to save now and buy later. There are certain people in this life who always assume someone else is going to pick up the tab. The parents' abdication of responsibility filters down to the next generation, and we end up with entire parts of the population who believe they don't have to work for anything because someone else will provide it. It is my firm belief that such an entitled attitude not only impacts our financial success but all aspects of our lives. Our physical, mental, and spiritual well-being are all tied to how we take responsibility for ourselves and our families.

Savings are particularly crucial today when pension benefits are being drastically reduced or even eliminated. Years ago, most employers offered a pension benefit, a fixed amount of money based on your years of service and salary, that you could not access until you retired. Such plans are quickly going by the wayside. Replacing them are 401(k) plans, which put most of the responsibility on the employee rather than the employer. Most companies match 401(k) contributions, which means free money, so taking advantage of that is imperative. Every time you change jobs, your 401(k) is impacted. Once you leave a job, chances are you will have several choices on what happens to your 401(k); you can sometimes leave it with the former employer, you can roll it into an IRA, or you can cash it out and pay taxes and potential penalties. Taking the cash may look appealing but is rarely the best thing to do. Keeping it in a tax-deferred account like an IRA or 401(k) is typically the better choice.

Consider the risk versus reward of where you put your savings. Generally, the higher the risk, the greater potential for reward. All investments are susceptible to being worth less a year from now, but some bear a greater risk than others. A US Treasury bond has much lower risk than a corporate bond. Consequently, the interest you receive from a corporate bond is generally higher than what you receive on a Treasury bond. Diversification limits the risk of something bad happening to your entire portfolio of investments, and there are many options out there. Diversification is very important, but as Warren Buffett famously said, "Diversification is protection against ignorance. It makes little sense if you know what you are doing." Bottom line: Do your homework, or trust your advisor to do it for you. Diversify, but don't delude yourself by believing buying multiple mutual funds is enough.

GET INVESTED

While there are thousands of books out there claiming the author has found the one system that will make us all rich, no such system exists. Riches come to those who patiently invest over a long period of time and in a broad range of investments, otherwise known as diversifying. There are so many different ways to invest and so many instruments to invest in that it can become extremely confusing for the average person to even begin. If you find yourself in this position, I suggest turning to a professional you trust while still educating yourself on the basics.

There are three basic investment categories. The first is stocks. A share of stock represents ownership in a corporation. For example, if a corporation has one million shares of stock outstanding, and you own one share, then you own one one-millionth of the company. Many companies' stocks are traded publicly on exchanges where shares can be bought and sold most any business day. When you buy a share of stock, you hope the value rises. Many people have done well investing in various companies' stocks. There is tremendous opportunity to find the next big thing, like Apple or Google. For example, if you had bought one hundred shares of Microsoft when it first became available to outside investors at the offering price of $21 per share, and sold it near its peak price around December 1,

1999, you would have parlayed that $2,100 into a profit of $1.4 million.

There are many similar stories of people who have made wise investments. However, there also is a considerable chance that the value of your investments will decline. Stock ownership is inherently risky. You are placing a bet on the success of one company.

The second investment category is bonds. A bond represents a loan that investors make to corporations and governments. Instead of giving up ownership through the sale of a share of stock, companies issue bonds that have to be paid back to the bondholder. In other words, if you buy a bond, you are lending money to the corporation or government entity just like a bank would. You receive interest over a period of time, which is called the term. At the end of the term, the corporation or government is obligated to pay you back if all goes well.

Just as people sometimes borrow money from banks that they cannot pay back, companies sometimes borrow money from bondholders that they ultimately cannot pay back. Under this unfortunate scenario, you then become a creditor of the company and hope there are enough assets to pay your principal amount. Oftentimes, there are not. Most reputable corporations pay their debts on time, but there is inherent risk in all investments, and bonds are no different.

Unless you plan to hold a bond until maturity, when the company pays off the loan you made to them, you can sell the bond as its value goes up and down. The price of the bond fluctuates oppositely from the direction of interest rates. If interest rates rise, the price of your bond goes down, and vice versa. If you sell a bond on the open market, the price you receive will be more or less than what you paid based on current interest rates. Bond prices also can change due to the financial health of the company, change in the status of the industry, a change in the law that impacts the company, and a host of other things. The market sets the price of bonds similar to the way stocks are priced.

The third investment category is also the most popular: mutual funds. Many of us invest in mutual funds through our 401(k)s or IRAs. A mutual fund is an investment company that purchases different stocks, bonds, and even other mutual funds. They then pool them together and sell shares of the combined group of investments. The investor benefits from a diversified portfolio, professional management, and liquidity of investment. There are dozens of subsets of mutual funds, and thousands of individual funds. According to Statistica.com, there were over nine thousand mutual funds in 2014 managing assets of nearly $16 trillion. Most of us benefit from investing in mutual funds rather than individual stocks and bonds because these companies are professional managers of money.

Determining which fund is right for you depends on your comprehensive financial plan. You must ask yourself how much risk you are willing to tolerate and consider when in your life you will need this money. Look into the fees associated with the funds you like and whether they have a sales charge or not. What's the track record of the fund and the company managing the fund? All of these questions and more are what you need to consider before investing in mutual funds.

Fees associated with mutual funds can have a huge impact on the amount of money you'll invest over time. The Annualized Return image shows the growth rate of an assumed 6.5 percent annualized return over thirty years. If you start out with a million dollars, a fund with a 3 percent fee grows to nearly $3 million. The same fund with a 2 percent fee grows to $3.7 million. A fund with a 1 percent fee grows to nearly $5 million. This shows how a relatively small fee can make a huge difference. Most mutual funds charge between 1 and 2 percent. Obviously it's important to pay attention to fees.

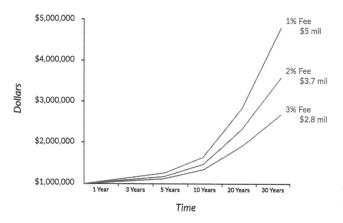

Assumed 6.5% Annualized Return over 30 Years

A more recent addition to investment options are ETFs, or exchange traded funds, which are similar to mutual funds but traded like stock and valued by the market minute by minute. Contrast this with mutual funds, which are valued at the end of the day at their closing. If you sell mutual fund shares at 11:00 a.m., you won't know the price you sold them at until the end of the day. With an ETF, once a buy or sell order is filled, you know the price.

REAL ESTATE

While the three previously discussed investments are those we hear the most about, there are many others. Other investment categories, including real estate, should be considered. Real estate investment trusts are like mutual funds except they invest in physical real estate like shopping centers, apartments, or other income-producing property. You acquire professional management of that investment without actually having to collect rents or maintain the property. It's an ideal way to invest in a particular kind of real estate that you could not otherwise buy on your own and don't have the expertise to manage by yourself.

Many people have been successful in buying residential rental properties, but it's not as easy as portrayed by those trying to sell books or seminars. For those with patience and discipline, investment in rental properties can pay handsome returns. It's also a great option for someone who's handy around the house and desires to start a part-time business. It's a popular way to diversify your income and your investments. Just remember: Despite the popularity of DIY flipping shows, it's not as easy as it looks. Before you invest in residential real estate, I suggest watching the great 1986 film *The Money Pit*. There's a reason that term is one we still use today.

If you live in an area that is rapidly expanding or developing, consider investing in transitional land. For someone with a long-term investment horizon and substantial cash in low-yielding investments, transitional land can be something to consider. Transitional land is in the path of commercial or residential development. The return is based on the appreciation of the raw land. There are typically no buildings to maintain, and while you're waiting for the land to appreciate, it can be leased for recreation or farming. One downside to transitional land is that it often takes a huge up-front sum of money to purchase and years until potential development arrives. If you have to finance anything on transitional land, it's important to be cognizant of interest costs.

Similar to transitional land is farmland. Farmland is often overlooked, but it is a hard asset and a hedge against inflation that, unlike precious metals such as gold and silver, pays a return through rental income from farmers. Farmland has outperformed many asset classes in the last fifty years with a return around 10 percent. In a world with a limited supply of farmable land and increasing demand for quality food, farmland can prove very valuable.

OTHER OPTIONS

Limited partnerships have several different subsets. There are oil and gas limited partnerships, as well as partnerships that concentrate on investing in movies and real estate. As with any investment, you need to understand the risk. Ask yourself if such an investment fits with your knowledge and understanding. You don't have to be an expert in what you're investing in, but you do need to understand the basics. In the mid-1980s, I invested in an oil and gas limited partnership. This was before my interest in money management and investing led me to further my education on such matters, and I really didn't understand what I was getting into. I didn't understand the fees, but I put my money into it anyway. At the end of the partnership, I got nothing back out of it other than a few tax deductions. I did not invest in any more oil and gas partnerships.

Limited partnerships require a relatively high income level. You have to be "qualified" to invest in them. Many are more sophisticated than what the average person can understand. They are not very liquid; in other words, there may not be an active market for selling them. I advise caution when considering a limited partnership.

CDs, or certificates of deposit, are far easier to understand. You can walk into a bank and buy a CD for a particular term from a few months to a few years. Current returns on CDs are very low, so they may not be attractive to most people. But if you need money in a relatively short period, then CDs or money market funds are a good option. There's not much risk, but there's also not much return.

Options and commodities are another investment category but can be very complicated. If you don't know what you're doing, you can open yourself up to unbelievable amounts of financial risk. In my opinion, it's best to steer clear of them. If you have a particular passion for them, I'd advise learning as much as you can about them and then invest with caution.

We hear a lot about investments in precious metals through the media. Gold, silver, and other metals are known to be a hedge against inflation. The value can go up as inflation goes up. Real estate can also serve as a hedge and pay a dividend through rental income. Precious metals can be purchased in lower increments than real estate and don't have the maintenance issues real estate can have. Having a relatively small percentage of your portfolio in inflations hedges is something you should consider.

When deciding how you will invest, make sure your choices align with your values. Ask yourself questions such as, "Do I care about whether the company I invest in manufactures tobacco products or produces drugs that terminate human life? Do I care how the company treats employees?" If you're not comfortable with a company's practices, avoid such investments, and find others you feel more at peace with. There are several good investment firms out there that can help you do just that, and the returns are comparable to those that invest based predominantly on only return. They can show you everything a company invests in, giving you all the information needed to determine if they are a good fit for you.

UNDERSTAND ANNUITIES

An annuity is an investment managed by an insurance company. It's a vehicle allowing you to invest either a lump sum or periodic investments for a specified term the investor chooses. At the end of the term, money is paid out in a lump sum or over several years.

It can be paid out over a person's lifetime or a joint lifetime. If a husband and wife have invested money in an annuity, it can be paid out over the lives of both. If one were to pass away, then the payment could continue. There are many different payment options. An annuity allows you to take a payment over a period of time guaranteed by the insurance company. For example, with an annuity without special premium refund features, if you put $100,000 into an annuity and start to take that money out over your lifetime, the insurance company will tell you, "Okay, you will receive X amount of dollars over your lifetime." Regardless of how long you live, whether it's five years or fifty years after you start those payments, the insurance company is obligated to pay you. Of course, they're placing a bet that you won't live as long as what projections indicated, in which case they get to keep the remaining part of your investment. For example, if you invested $100,000 and lived for two years and there was $80,000 left in that account, that $80,000 would go back to the insurance company and would not go to your heirs.

There are upsides and downsides to annuities. Annuities can have heavy fees involved, known in the business as "surrender charges." If you invested using the example of $100,000 and need that money a year later, the insurance company will charge you a fee for taking money out early. Fees can be as high as 8 percent, but they decrease over time. After so many years, the surrender charge drops to zero, and you may be able to withdraw your money at will.

Think of annuities as you would any investment vehicle, and know the details. Understand the fees. Oftentimes, a salesperson will explain the charges and fees, but when an emergency hits and the buyer needs money, the buyer is surprised by how much less he or she is able to access. When you put money into an annuity, you aren't assuming you're going to need it soon. They're typically long-term investments, and they need to be treated as such.

Within annuities, there are many different options.

Variable annuities invest in mutual funds, and the value fluctuates with the market. Fixed annuities can come with a guaranteed or variable rate of return depending on the product. In all cases, an insurance company is guaranteeing your payment, not a bank and not the government. It's important to understand all options before you invest in any annuity, particularly in regard to how they fit within your comprehensive financial plan.

RULES FOR INVESTING

1. Use an investment most appropriate for what you're saving for. For instance, don't invest emergency fund money in the stock market. Put it in an easy-to-get-to money market fund that won't fluctuate in price. On the other hand, if you're twenty-five years old, a money market fund at the bank is probably not the best place to invest for the long term.

2. Invest automatically. Make your wealth grow automatically through payroll deductions or withdrawals from a bank account put directly into an investment account. Applying the principle of "dollar cost averaging" over a long period of time, ensures that you are purchasing more shares when prices are lower and fewer when prices are higher, which is exactly what you should be doing.

3. Diversify your savings in investments. You've heard the

saying, "Don't put all your eggs in one basket." The same goes for investments. Some investments, like mutual funds, are automatically diversified when it comes to investing in different companies, but be careful. Just because you invest in one mutual fund doesn't mean you're properly diversified across investment classes.

4. Never invest in something you don't understand. That doesn't mean you have to be an expert, but you need to at least have a cursory knowledge of what you're investing in. If you don't understand anything about the oil and gas business and don't understand how the partnership works, it's probably not the right investment for you.

5. Remember that if it sounds too good to be true, then it probably is. With few exceptions, the only way to get rich is to work harder and smarter and follow the rules of this book. You probably won't find the next Microsoft, but if you do, you have to know when to sell. Selling is often a more difficult decision than buying.

6. Invest in yourself first, which you already are doing simply by reading this book. You don't have to go back to school for an advanced degree to learn a new skill. Check out your local library, a community college, or certification programs like I did to become a CFP®. Taking up any of those options means you're investing in yourself. Even reading the *Wall Street Journal* or a blog on personal finance betters your understanding of how this all works.

BONUS RULE: DON'T ALWAYS BELIEVE WHAT YOU SEE, HEAR, OR READ

One of the reasons I wrote this book is because of the vast amount of misinformation about the subject of personal finance. Much of this misinformation comes from financial reporters and commentators who have little if any background in the products they purport to know so much about. They become emboldened by the fact that the regulatory bodies overseeing licensing of legitimate advisors exempt those who don't give specific financial advice or are merely "educating" the masses. People read a few things on the Internet and deem themselves as informed as people who have devoted entire careers to the fields. If you're a dynamic speaker, clever blogger, or happen to know a good marketing professional, you can present yourself as an "expert" in most any field.

Many of these people become victims of their own lazy or nonexistent analysis. They oftentimes repeat something they've heard or read and change it just enough to call it their own. They do no independent analysis, use outdated material, or rely on misinformation from another nonexpert, which results in perpetuated myths. Over time, their voices grow louder, and because they appear to be coming from legitimate, trusted, high-profile "personalities," the public begins to think what they say must be true.

One of the most derided and mischaracterized products is variable annuities. Our firm does make variable annuities available to clients when it's in their best interests. But there are bad actors in every professional arena, and those who sell investment products, including variable annuities, are no different. Whenever you hear someone say categorically that a particular financial vehicle is "always bad," ask a lot of questions. Words like "always" and "never" should be a dog whistle to you that someone is selling you a bill of goods.

The perceived vices surrounding variable annuities tend to get a lot of press and discussion from widely published financial gurus, including many who are not licensed to give financial advice. One of the most common myths involves the annual costs of a variable annuity when compared to mutual funds. Mutual funds are believed, on average, to have annual expenses around 1.5 percent, while variable annuities check in at 2.3 to 2.7 percent. So why would you buy a variable annuity when you could buy a mutual fund at a lower annual cost? You would because, as John P. Huggard points out in the tenth edition of his book *The Truth About Variable Annuities*, mutual funds have annual expenses closer to 5 percent once taxes and sales charges are incorporated.

People often also associate hefty surrender charges with

variable annuities, which can be a harsh reality. Variable annuities can cost you big if you withdraw your money before the surrender charges expire—up to 8 percent in the first year and decreasing over the remaining six years. This is where a qualified financial professional with no commission or sales fee to gain can help. If you're going to need your money from a variable annuity with high surrender fees within the first few years after you invest, this is a product unsuitable for your needs. If a salesperson tries to sell you such a product knowing you'll soon need the money, find another advisor. An ethical financial advisor that is bound by SEC and FINRA rules will not sell you such a product.

A variable annuity is nothing more than a contract with an insurance company that allows the purchaser to buy investments within what are called subaccounts. The investments are similar to mutual funds and, like mutual funds, vary in investment type and goal. The word "variable" comes into play because the investments "vary" in value day to day, just like the value of mutual funds, thus the value fluctuates depending on the market value.

Sometimes, the word "deferred" is used in conjunction with variable annuities. This refers to tax deferral, the biggest advantage of variable annuities. Any growth over and above the original investment is not taxed until withdrawn, which allows for tax-deferred compounding. Depending on the particular variable annuity, there can be other benefits, such as value floors guaranteeing your investment will never decrease in value, death benefits, income riders, long-term care benefits, and more.

If there is a financial product or investment that appears to meet your needs, I urge that you:

1. Don't automatically believe the salesman.
2. Don't automatically believe what you read on the Internet.
3. Don't automatically take the advice of your brother-in-law or friend. Your situation is different from anyone else's.
4. Seek out a trusted advisor who is not a salesman to confirm that the product is legitimate.

GET READY TO RETIRE

When planning for retirement, you first need to know when you plan to do it and what kind of income stream you will require. Look at what you've invested to determine if it will met your needs. Consider your family's longevity and your risk adverseness, and commit to a plan that works for you.

While the most prevalent options for retirement planning

include investing in 401(k)s and IRAs, there are variations of them. Most are tax-favored plans, meaning you typically put money in before you pay taxes on it. Once you start to withdraw that money, you pay income tax on it. When you make an investment in a Roth IRA or a Roth-style 401(k), you pay income tax up-front. It's tax-free when you withdraw it. This is a great option for a younger person just starting out, as that money grows tax free over the rest of your investment career.

Contrary to popular belief, 401(k)s and IRAs are plans, not investments. They act as "containers" for types of investments. Many times, people say they are "investing in their 401(k) or IRA." In a 401(k), investments are typically limited by the plan sponsor. They are usually several different types and classes of mutual funds. In an IRA, you have a much broader range of investments. People even invest in farmland, businesses, and gold in IRAs. The only prohibited investments are insurance policies and art.

If you work for a school or nonprofit organization, a 403(b) plan is similar to a 401(k) in that you can invest money before tax and withdraw it at your discretion. A 457 plan is a tax-deferred plan available to governmental employees. Salary deferral plans are available to some high-salaried employees, but I advise caution when dealing with them.

There typically is no guarantee that if the company has financial problems or declares bankruptcy, the deferral will be honored.

Anytime you have the ability to invest in a company's savings or 401(k) plan and the company will match your investment up to certain levels, take advantage. Consider it free money. A company I worked at for many years had a 401(k) plan that allowed you to invest up to 6 percent of your salary and matched your contributions dollar for dollar. The company didn't offer a traditional pension plan any longer, so management encouraged employees to save for their retirement or other goals. Those who chose not to invest the full 6 percent were leaving money on the table.

There also are plans for the self-employed or those who work for small companies that don't offer plans. The rules and investment limits for all tax-advantaged plans are updated every year. The IRS has extensive material online explaining these rules and limits. Also check with your tax professional or financial planner on which plan may be best for your situation.

GET SOCIAL

For many of us, one of the largest sources of cash in

retirement will come from our Social Security benefit. For the last three decades, many have ridiculed the system for being underfunded, woefully troubled, and on the verge of bankruptcy, yet it remains the primary source of income for most people entering traditional retirement. Projections show the system is funded into the 2030s. Undoubtedly, there will be changes to the benefits in the future, but for now, Social Security should be one of the three legs your retirement stool is composed of, along with tax-deferred plans such as 401(k)s and IRAs and personal savings and income.

While Social Security is not an investment, it pays like one by providing monthly income. It is perhaps one of the most misunderstood and misapplied government programs available to citizens. It is imperative that you know the basics of how benefits are paid, as failure to understand the nuances of the program can result in ill-informed choices and thousands of dollars of missed benefits. Your first step should be a visit to SSA.gov where you can request an estimate of your benefit. Next, take some time to understand exactly how your benefit works. There are many books and online tools to help you through the maze of requirements and regulations. A personal favorite is *Social Security: The Inside Story* by Andy Landis.

The retirement benefits Social Security offers start at age

sixty-two with a few exceptions. For example, widows are eligible at age sixty and disabled widows at age fifty. Starting your benefit payments at age sixty-two may sound great, but there are ramifications to consider. You must ask yourself what you will have to give up by starting so early and, conversely, what you can gain by waiting. What impact does your spouse have on your benefit? What kind of health are you in, and what kind of longevity runs in your family? There are several sources available to better understand how the answers to these questions will impact your benefit. Also important to keep in mind is Rule One in this book: Create a Comprehensive Financial Plan. Social Security is only one element of your financial life. A holistic look at all elements should be considered when formulating the best plan for you.

See the glossary of investment terms in this book's appendix for further reference. I leave you with this. When it comes to saving and investing, many people try to outguess the market. The chart on the following page tells us we are foolish to do so. Be patient and stay the course. The seemingly dire situation today will change and history tells us it will usually change for the better.

Timing the Market is Risky and Rarely Works

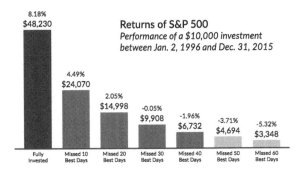

Returns of S&P 500
Performance of a $10,000 investment between Jan. 2, 1996 and Dec. 31, 2015

Six of the 10 best days occured within two weeks of the 10 worst days

source: www.cheatsheet.com

Rule Seven

START A BUSINESS

"The only thing that stands between a man and what he wants from life is often merely the will to try it and the faith to believe that it is possible."

—RICHARD DEVOS, COFOUNDER OF AMWAY

Most of us plan on slowing down or retiring someday. Most of us also have hobbies we enjoy outside of work. As we approach retirement age, we must ask ourselves what we intend to do with our newfound free time. It presents an ideal opportunity to explore your passions and determine the role they can play in helping you achieve your goals.

Starting a business can be part of anyone's comprehensive

financial plan. When considering starting one, think about what your true mission will be. Aside from making money, perhaps you want to help your family or community. The right kind of business can help you do that. You can impart your values on others while gaining life experience and a better understanding of how the world works. If nothing else, it will help you stay focused and optimistic in the later years of your life.

One of the great benefits of starting a business is the extra income. Another is the role it can play in keeping you active and fulfilled. Many studies have been written about the benefits of staying busy for a lifetime. We've all heard stories of people who retired from big corporations after thirty-five years and had no plans other than to go fishing. Very quickly, they become bored, possibly even depressed, and their health declines. Most of us still have plenty of life left in us after retirement, and starting a small business can be the perfect way to remain active while continuing to hone our skills.

Starting a business also can provide peace of mind after you leave a full-time position. When you give up a regular job, certain connections become severed. Both your network of contacts and the daily feeling of accomplishment suddenly go away. Even if you hated your job, you likely still made relationships along the way that helped sustain you. While you might maintain some of those friendships outside of work, the ties that bind are gone.

Retirement also often changes one's attitude about investing, as the regular income stream stops. It's common for people to become blinded by the need for passive income, and therefore become overly cautious and conservative in their investment decisions. One of the biggest mistakes people entering retirement make is failing to recognize that passive income from investments can take a negative turn. We tend to assume our investments will be sufficient to maintain the lifestyle we want, and the realization that that might not be the case can result in deep anxiety.

Starting a profitable business or finding a part-time job allows you to remain active beyond day-to-day survival. If you're young and just beginning your career, starting a business is likely the farthest thing from your mind, but I strongly urge you to consider planning for it early. Active income allows you to depend less on passive sources while helping you preserve a sense of self-worth.

DO WHAT YOU LOVE

As you look to your future, don't even think of continuing to work a job you hate. Find something different, and understand that work can be fulfilling when you combine it with a mission and passion. When deciding what type of business to start, allow yourself to think outside the box. I know a fireman who went on to become a pumpkin grower and who is now one of the biggest wholesale suppliers in the central part of our state. He does it part-time, and he absolutely loves it. He and his family run a pumpkin outlet where people can drive by and pick up pumpkins in the fall. He also supplies many stores in the area and serves some of the large grocery chains.

The possibilities truly are endless, especially in this age of ever-expanding technology. There is great demand right now for website builders. Or perhaps you have an idea for a blog. No matter your skill set, you can parlay your unique knowledge into something profitable. Find a passion, play to your strengths, and build your business around them. Do you have a big backyard? Consider planting a garden and going to your local farmers' market with fresh vegetables and flowers. Do you like cooking or have a special baked good that people rave about? Many states have an exception for commercial kitchen requirements for baked goods sold at farmers' markets. Do you like working with crafts, wood, or collectibles? There are countless projects you can tackle and sell online—Etsy and eBay are great outlets to market such projects. Learn as much as you can about the field that interests you, and dive in.

My family started our own popcorn business a few years ago (www.groomsvillepopcorn.com). We grew tired of mowing the grass on our property, so we planted part of the yard in popcorn, got a huge yield, and started selling kernels as well as ears, and we popped popcorn at the local farmers' market. We don't make a lot of money, but we have a lot of fun doing it as a family. It helps the kids understand the benefits of a business and how return is based solely on the effort we put into it.

Even if it seems profitable, steer clear of starting a business in a field you hate. If you don't want to be in the service industry, don't buy a McDonald's franchise. Instead, tie your business into your life mission. Find the intersection between your expertise and the needs of others. You don't need an MBA, a formal business plan, or even employees. All you need is a product or service that springs from something you love to do.

If it's a business that doesn't require much money to start, there's little risk. If it is more consuming, both from a time and a financial standpoint, it might require more due diligence. Consider the investment required, and include it in your comprehensive financial plan. Make sure you understand the business and the capital requirements to start it, then plan, save, and, eventually, have fun with it.

REMAIN REALISTIC

Building a business can be difficult. If your family is involved, it can be even tougher. Family businesses rarely last beyond the second generation because everyone has their own ideas of how the business should be run. Unless founders are willing to teach others the keys to running a successful operation, that knowledge typically leaves this earth with them. If business owners want to pass along their business, they must be teachers at heart and pass down their experiences to the younger generations. It's also important to remember that no one person has all the answers. Others in the family likely have their own good ideas and should be allowed to contribute. Owners who have a hard time communicating with their family and employees about the business tend to want to control rather than collaborate. If you are one of these people, force yourself to sit down on a regular basis to discuss the business with all those involved and make sure everyone feels valued and respected. You won't be around forever, and preparing the next generation to take on the business is as important as growing it. In some cases, young family members work in the business before going off to college. When they return home with newfound knowledge that could help improve the way the business functions, their suggestions are dismissed, much to the detriment of the entire operation. Granted, not every idea should be implemented, but each should be given proper consideration.

When starting a business, it helps if you have experienced the working world from the perspective of an employee firsthand. Many times, people who start their work lives as business owners have a difficult time understanding the employee perspective. There's an entire television show dedicated to the employer's lack of understanding when it comes to the people who are truly making his or her business a success: *Undercover Boss*. It's amazing what the boss finds out once he or she is working alongside frontline employees. Oftentimes, those employees know more than the boss does. Someone who spends all their days at headquarters can't see the day-to-day struggles of the workforce.

If you can make a business work, there are tax savings to be had. While you pay taxes on the income it produces, growth of the value of the business is sheltered. For instance, you can hire your kids and deduct their pay from your profits. Oftentimes, things needed for a business are also used in daily life, and the business-use portion of those expenses can be deducted. There are deductions for vehicles used for work. You also can start a tax-deferred IRA-type savings plan just for the business based on the income generated.

STEPS FOR STARTING A SUCCESSFUL BUSINESS

1. *Write a business plan.* This sounds simple, but not doing so can be the reason some good businesses never get off the ground. Some people are petrified of the thought of putting together a detailed plan. I urge you to relax and understand that you are allowed to be flexible. If you're considering a part-time or low-cost business, the important thing is to get the business started. Your plan can evolve over time. You will have plenty of time to fill in the gaps as you gain experience. If your plan involves a large investment or substantial loans from a bank, you have less wiggle room. If you're spending that kind of money, both you and the bank need to have a good indication that you will be successful. In my family's situation, we had an idea and relatively minor expectations. For our leap into our popcorn business, we didn't commit a large amount of money to the endeavor and remained flexible in changing product types, purchasing equipment, and expanding into additional markets. Ours was and still is a part-time business, and while we dream about someday going full-time, we realize a more formal plan will be necessary to do so.

2. *Learn all you can about the business.* Many people plunge into a business without understanding all the different aspects of it. There is much to consider, including the market, competitors, start-up and sustainability funds,

time requirement, location, inventory, advertising, and much more. The best way to learn what starting any business entails is to work in the field for someone else. If you want to start a restaurant, work in one first. Work in as many aspects as possible, including sales, production, marketing, and purchasing. Even if you're buying into a franchise, work in it first. While my family had no experience on the retail side of popcorn selling, we had grown popcorn for a major brand name based on a contractual growing arrangement. They furnished the seed, and we provided them the resulting crop. We were paid based on the number of tons produced. They processed the raw popcorn and packaged it into the various products you see on the shelf. We quickly discovered that the cost to produce popcorn is relatively small compared to the cost and effort in processing, packaging, and getting it onto store shelves, to the farmers' market, or to the customer's home via ordering on our website. Each one of those sales channels was unique and presented its own challenges, and we continue to learn something new learn every day.

3. *Choose a location.* If you're going to have a storefront, location is extremely important. Starting a bookstore in a country town of five hundred is probably not going to serve you well unless you make it a destination. The more straightforward route is to research the areas

you're interested in, analyze your key demographics, and determine the availability of rentable space. The old adage "location, location, location" is absolutely true. If you're going to depend on a traditional storefront, do your research. If you can start a business without a storefront, do so. There are many businesses that don't require renting space and buying business furniture. Because my family operates our business part-time with very low overhead, we decided early on that a storefront just didn't make economic sense. It could someday, but for now, we rely on farmers' markets, website sales, and third-party retail locations to sell our product. As our reputation grows, we believe the demand will increase through each of these channels.

4. *Market everywhere.* Note that I didn't say "advertise." Marketing is more personal in that you're putting your reputation on the line with a product or service that people may not want, but it's your job to convince them that they need it. This might sound counterintuitive to my advice on understanding needs versus wants in previous chapters, but in this case, you're the seller and your "need" is to make an income. It's never okay to sacrifice your integrity for the sake of a buck by starting a business that doesn't match your values. We believe popcorn is one of the few healthy snacks left. The rise in childhood obesity, diabetes,

and other diet-related illnesses is appalling, and our business fits nicely into our goal of providing a healthy and nutritious snack for the entire family. One of our first marketing efforts was at the farmers' market. We sold kernels for five dollars in a two-pound bag, which is more than what you'll pay in the supermarket, but customers like that we grow locally and that they can actually talk to the people behind the business. However, selling only kernels severely limited our sales volume, and we had to expand our product line to include something that customers would come back for week after week. We came up with a unique twist on microwave popcorn that allows customers to pop the popcorn directly off the ear. In addition, we started selling bags of popped popcorn in resealable bags. We weren't bashful about pricing our product at the high end, because we believe we supply a superior quality product when compared to the mass produced and marketed popcorn products. Never be afraid to charge a high price for a product. I've seen vendors at farmers' markets try to compete on price, and it is an ultimate race to the bottom. If you find yourself in that position, rethink your pricing strategy or business model. Higher priced products are sold, not bought. You have to be willing to communicate with your customer and understand what's important to them.

5. *Finance your business.* Save your seed money, and be

your own bank. The number-one cause of failure for new businesses is lack of capital through the start-up phase. Make sure your concept has a chance before you risk your financial future with a business that just isn't workable. We financed our popcorn business ourselves. We were already sitting on the most difficult assets to acquire, the land and a building for processing. Our initial outlay for seed, fertilizer, and other inputs was fairly minimal. We already had access to planting equipment and a tractor. We hired a farmer neighbor to harvest our crop the first year with his combine. Our biggest expense the first year was processing the kernels once harvested. We had to construct a small-scale grain dryer from scratch. In the next few years, we purchased a commercial popcorn popper for our popped product and then a mechanical harvester to alleviate the backbreaking labor of handpicking and the associated costs of such an effort.

6. *Make sure you are legal.* This means securing licenses, paying local and state taxes, complying with all laws and ordinances, and obtaining insurance, among other requirements. People who try to fly under the radar only end up getting burned. Pay particular attention to laws and ordinances if you're trying to sell anything food-related. Laws vary widely depending on locale, and every situation is unique. In our case, we had to learn about the tax laws that apply to selling our

product retail. There is no sales tax if you sell only the kernels, but once you pop it, it is taxed. We chose to price the product with the tax included. Every month, we have to make a filing with the state regarding how much taxable product we sold and pay the tax. Because we sell a ready-to-eat product, we had to look into the food-safety requirements for our locale. When we sold only at farmers' markets, regulations were minimal. Once we started selling on a wholesale basis, the regulations became more demanding. Liability insurance for our product also is a must. Being sued for millions of dollars should someone get hurt or sick while consuming a four-dollar bag of popcorn is not worth the risk.

7. *Decide how to handle your business's logos, stationery, website design, and legal structure.* This is all important, but don't let it stand in your way of getting started. Some people get so hung up on the exact colors the logo needs to be or the kind of office furniture to buy, they miss the bigger picture. We didn't start out in the popcorn business with any of these things in place. We added them later after we determined we had a viable product. For most of it, I recommend seeking out the experts. In order to get quality services, you need to expect to pay for the expertise. We paid a freelance web designer a flat rate for design, optimization, and storefront for our site. For occasional

tweaks, he charges an hourly rate. When deciding on your business's legal structure, seek the help of an attorney, whether online or in person. We went with a local attorney, because, as previously mentioned, I prefer in-person interaction.

8. *Take a course.* Educate yourself, online or otherwise, on what goes into starting a business. The U.S. Small Business Administration has several online resources to get you started. I encourage you to visit SBA.gov for more information. There might also be free or low-cost resources available in your local area to assist you. Seek these out to help give you a better understanding. I helped run the family farm operation for years, which gave me a basic understanding of accounting, taxes, and the physical requirements for planting, caring for, and harvesting a crop. Traditional farmers who grow commodity crops don't do a great deal of marketing to end users. There are a limited number of wholesale buyers for your crop. Taking a plunge into retail is a completely different situation. We have learned how to best market and serve the end-use customer. The biggest learning curve came when we embarked on the process of getting product on the shelves of a major chain grocery. It takes a major time commitment to complete all the back-office requirements, but once you're in, you're in, and you can gain valuable exposure for your product. Depending on your product,

the retail merchant might also provide assistance. Because we grow a local product, and grocery chains like to tout that they sell locally produced items, we found them to be very helpful and encouraging along the way.

Rule Eight

MANAGE, ENJOY, GIVE

"You have not lived today until you have done something for someone who can never repay you."

—JOHN BUNYAN, ENGLISH WRITER

Wealth management is never static. It is a lifelong, active process with many moving pieces. In Rule One: Create a Comprehensive Financial Plan, we outlined all the elements of a comprehensive financial plan with the understanding that life happens and our circumstances change. Our obligations change. We change jobs, children are born, opportunities to start a business present themselves—the list is endless. These changes might not alter our goals, but they can affect the manner by which we achieve them.

Just as any long road trip requires taking the occasional detour around construction or accidents, our financial plan must allow us to navigate around life's obstacles. Determining the best route around such obstacles requires regular reevaluation of our plan. Ongoing management with or without a financial advisor is perhaps the most overlooked part of creating a financial plan. You cannot simply stick the plan in the drawer and expect it to do all the work for you. You have to work the plan and review it regularly.

As you head toward a place of financial security, it becomes time to think about what type of spending will give you joy. Maybe it means having enough money in retirement to do the things you want. Perhaps it's considering your next vacation. Think about charitable giving, the causes you can support and who will benefit. For many of us, the day-to-day grind has kept us from thinking about what we would do if we achieved financial success. Now is the time to consider all options.

While the future is unknown, putting boundaries around possible outcomes can give you comfort. There might be certain things that are constantly on your mind regarding the future, and while it's important to keep thinking about those things, finding a place of comfort or peace of mind is crucial to your long-term joy. A financial plan gives you the guidance to deal with any scenario and can even present solutions you never thought possible.

HOW WILL YOU BE REMEMBERED?

Our legacies are the most important thing we leave behind when we move on to the afterlife. What our loved ones remember about us ultimately defines the meaning of our lives. Working toward a legacy provides perspective on the future and forces us to look at the impact we have on those around us.

We all know you get back far more than you give when you're generous with your time, talents, and treasures. There is a particular joy that comes from giving, especially to those in need, and the far-reaching impact of an act of kindness can be immeasurable. I know of a family that goes to the local Kmart every year during the holidays. They go to the layaway counter and ask if any of the orders consist mostly of toys and children's clothing. They then pay off the remainder of the balance anonymously on that order. They do this for as many layaway orders as they can afford. They are bringing joy to people they have never and will never meet. It might seem like a small thing, but acts of generosity and compassion don't have to be grand. We are all called to a greater good and to be examples to others through our giving. Grace, defined as "unmerited favor," has been provided to us in many different ways. What a wonderful feeling to provide a small taste of that amazing grace to others.

Anybody can give, even if you're one of the many people just trying to make it by day to day. Try to set aside a small portion. Every dollar dropped in the church collection plate or Salvation Army kettle counts. It brings such satisfaction to help someone in need, even when we don't have much on our own. Here in America, even the least among us has more than most people in third-world countries. It's important to realize just how much we truly have been blessed with and to consider the circumstances of others. Giving is a part of life. As long as we treat it as such, we will be blessed accordingly. I believe we are all called to a higher purpose, and building riches is not about having everything we want today but leaving behind a legacy for our families, churches, communities, and country.

I hope these rules have motivated you to better prepare for your financial future. While they're not difficult to grasp, they can be challenging to execute. For most of us, the only thing blocking the path to financial freedom is our own behavior. Success ultimately depends on discipline and delaying gratification for a greater cause.

While it might not always be easy to see, there is an order

to God's plan for us. Everything from humans to plants to animals to land is connected in His plan. We seek to establish that same sense of order in our own lives. We can't control everything around us, but we can make the world a better place by leaving less chaos. Making a financial plan and sticking with it can help us find the peace and stability we so desperately crave.

One of my favorite verses in the Bible is Jeremiah 29:11: "For I know the plans I have for you, said the Lord. Plans for your welfare and not for harm. To give you a future with hope." Jeremiah's sole purpose was to reveal the sins of the people and explain the reason for the impending disaster about to come upon them. These are God's words to a people who have been torn from their homeland, their Temple, and their king. They are seemingly hopeless.

God's word gives us a glimpse into the future, and from them, we learn that it's best not to dwell on the immediate dire circumstances, but rather to work expediently through our difficulties. In every desperate situation, there is a brighter view on the other side. I believe God's plan for us is filled with goodness and grace. But we must be an active participant in it and manage our lives in such a way that we can care for the people, community, and environment around us.

Conclusion

As a young adult, I embarked on the trip of a lifetime. The events leading me to such a journey were set in motion when I was just a child. I lost my dad to an early death when I was eight years old. I had three older brothers who kept me busy on the farm and gave me occasional guidance when Mom didn't know what to do, but they weren't Dad. I missed out on so much he could have offered me and felt a great void in his absence. He was never able to impart upon me his wisdom gained from growing up with twelve siblings in the hills of Appalachia. I heard no firsthand accounts of his time spent hunting, fishing, and eking out a living farming the soil. As humans, we thrive on stories, and I longed to hear Dad's. Because of this deep need to better understand him, I sought out my own adventure and set off on what would become a life-changing story of my own.

Over the summer between my junior and senior years in college, I rode a bicycle three thousand miles coast to coast. A group of sixty-five of us dipped our back tires in the Pacific Ocean and rode an average of one hundred miles a day for six weeks. We camped outside, occasionally stayed in churches and schools, and even more occasionally were able to take a shower.

Prior to this trip, I had spent summers working on the farm to earn money to go to school and drive nice cars. This particular summer, I remember thinking about Dad and the adventures he had as a young man that I would never know about. I yearned for some adventure of my own before I was thrust into a career. As a twenty-two-year-old, I also wasn't very aware of other people's circumstances or feelings. Empathy and compassion were largely foreign concepts. Like many young men that age, I was rather self-centered and more concerned about the car I was driving than generosity. Little did I know, this trip would change me in ways I could never imagine, mile by mile, one life lesson at a time.

At the onset of the trip, we traveled by bus westward on some of the same roads we would be riding back east, and I soon began to believe I had made a grave mistake. A bike and full duffle bag were the only possessions we could bring. We had a seemingly unfathomable task ahead of us. I wondered who among us would break. Would it be me? How could someone relatively out of shape make it through California deserts in the middle of summer and over Colorado mountain passes in excess of thirteen thousand feet? Looking back, I realize this was the trip's first life lesson: Anticipation often makes our challenges seem much worse than they really are.

We rode with the goal of arriving at our destination as a team rather than individually. This took some getting used to for me. I preferred to make due on my own, remain independent, and never rely on anyone else to survive. I quickly learned such an impatient, selfish mentality is of no use when taking on a feat like this one. Contrary to what many self-help books teach us, we desperately need each other. We spent a lot of time waiting for people to catch up, but we took the opportunity to rest, enjoy our surroundings, and just talk. This was life lesson number two: Sometimes it is better to listen more than speak, watch more than perform, and wait more than rush. If we combine all those, we just may be able to exercise the patience to investigate the needs of others and not simply turn a blind eye to their struggles.

Anyone who has ridden a long distance on a bicycle knows how painful it can become to sit down. My fellow riders assured me that I would get used to it after about ten days. I did, but that week and a half was utter misery. It was enough to make me second-guess myself. I was convinced I had made a terrible mistake. My mind began telling me things that seemed to be true but weren't. "This really won't get better, and this misery will be with you the entire trip," it said. "You just need to pack it in and call it a day," it goaded. But as the pain began gradually to subside, I learned life lesson number three: No matter your circumstances, pain is a temporary condition. As the Bible reads in James 1:2–3, "Consider it pure joy, my brothers and sisters, whenever you face trials of many kinds, because you know that the testing of your faith produces perseverance. Let perseverance finish its work so that you may be mature and complete, not lacking anything."

The joy of conquering a mountain with a bicycle for the first time is hard to overstate. The serenity of taking in the beauty of creation while at the same time experiencing extreme exhaustion is a strange dichotomy. Here was life lesson number four: Exhilaration comes after the climb, after the pain, and after the effort. Hard work and effort always precede the reward.

At one point on the trip, nearly every one of us fell ill from shigellosis, an extreme form of food poisoning caused by a bad batch of tuna salad. Our symptoms were so severe that our long caravan of bikes was stopped cold in our tracks in a little Arkansas town called Cotton Plant. I was one of the first to get sick and spent three days in the hospital. At first, doctors thought I suffered from heat stroke—after all, we had just traveled nearly two thousand miles in the middle of July through some of the hottest weather on record. They administered an ice bath, one of the worst experiences in my life. It lowered my 105-degree temperature, but only for a moment. Finally, they came to the correct diagnosis, and heavy doses of antibiotics and fluids brought me and the others back to life. This was life lesson number five: Take nothing for granted. Life is robust, yet fragile. Your health, your wealth, and your relationships can all change in a flash. Be prepared to face the challenges of life, as they certainly will come.

At this point, we still had eight hundred miles to complete, and I was determined to finish. As we crossed the bridge over the river into Mississippi, I felt as if we were starting our trip from the beginning. Our momentum was lost. All of us were still on heavy antibiotics, and doctors warned that we were highly susceptible to sunburn as a side effect of the medicine. We had to cover up with long-sleeved shirts for the rest of the trip. We banned together and persevered, staying the course and never giving up until we finally arrived at our destination in Fernandina Beach, Florida. We made it there slightly past our projected arrival date, but we were intact and elated. A local television station chronicled our arrival along with a short story on the trials of our journey. The sense of achievement I felt that day remains strong in my heart and taught me life lesson number six: Success is achieved through sacrifice, but more importantly, perseverance; and instant gratification can never compare.

Through every trial, tribulation, and victory, my trip taught me that a vital part of our mission on this earth is to maximize compassion. From the relationships I forged with my fellow riders to the people I met in every Smalltown, USA, I began to understand the importance we all play in each other's lives. Compassion is defined as concern for the sufferings and misfortune of others. It is more than empathy—it's empathy in action. Any riches we receive in this life are meant to be shared with those who need them most. We must be aware of the needs of others and how any suffering can be alleviated. Compassion is a trait tough to learn without experiencing the world, but it's one we all should strive to master.

Every lesson learned along my trip can be applied to your own journey to financial freedom. Do not be afraid to take on the task. Do not expect to do it alone. Understand that the truly difficult part is only temporary, and any setback can be overcome. Never take anything for granted, and prepare for all scenarios. Enjoy the rewards of your hard work.

And, most importantly, never forget to use your success to help better the world around you.

Appendix

EXPLANATION OF MUTUAL FUNDS

WHAT IS A MUTUAL FUND?

A mutual fund is a company that invests in stocks, bonds, and other securities. When your money is in a mutual fund, you own shares in those funds that in turn own shares of stocks, bonds, and other securities. You can earn profits in several ways. Periodic distributions can come from capital gains and dividends or an overall rise in the price of the mutual fund shares. Much like any investment, there is risk, as share prices frequently rise and fall.

PROS

The best thing about an actively managed mutual fund is that someone else is doing all the hard work for you at a very reasonable rate. You don't have to do any of the research or buying and selling.

Mutual funds also offer diversity for your portfolio. As we all know, you shouldn't put all your eggs in one basket. Mutual funds allow you to invest in many stocks or other securities at various companies ranging in size and scope.

Mutual funds also offer liquidity because they are bought and sold similarly to stocks. You can trade them in for cash at your discretion.

Investing in mutual funds is simple and doesn't require a huge up-front expense. Some minimums are as low as twenty-five dollars.

CONS

Some people don't want others managing their money. In this case, the first pro becomes a con. It's understandable, especially if you've been burned in the past, but in my opinion, seeking out professional help always is the best course of action.

Another con is one word: fees. You pay for them, and they can hurt your gains. They vary from fund to fund, so make sure you know what you're getting into.

If the funds are not in a tax-deferred account, taxes can be a burden. It's considered a taxable event every time a fund manager sells a stock. Gains are taxed regardless of whether you received a distribution of cash or not.

SOME TYPES OF MUTUAL FUNDS

Money market funds are generally the safest but have the lowest returns. They include short-term debt instruments, Treasury bills, and short-term corporate securities.

Income funds aim to bring in a steady source of cash from the interest on the government and corporate bonds they own. However, they can drop in value when underlying bonds or notes they invest in decrease in value.

Balanced funds offer a mix of safety and risk. They invest in a combination of bonds and equities. The weight of investment in each area depends on the asset class. Similarly, asset allocation funds have the same objective but do not have to hold a specified percentage of any asset class.

Equity funds invest in stocks and represent the largest category of mutual funds. Generally, the investment objective of this class of funds is long-term capital growth with some income. There are, however, many different types of equity funds because there are many different types of equities.

A **global fund** invests anywhere internationally; an **international fund** invests only outside the country where you live. These funds tend to be more risky, and conditions vary from country to country, but these types of investments can be a nice way to balance a portfolio.

Specialty funds concentrate on certain segments of the economy. **Sector funds** include areas such as finance, technology, and health and can carry great risk should the sector begin to fail. **Regional funds** allow you to buy stock in foreign countries but are sensitive to fundamental political or economic shifts in the particular country.

When you invest in **socially responsible and faith-based funds,** you're putting your money in companies that are in line with your personal values. Industries that are often avoided in these funds include tobacco, alcohol, weapons, and other industries the investor wishes to avoid.

An **index fund** merely replicates the overall market return in the form of investing in a broad market index such as the S&P 500. There is no need for professional management of the portfolio, since the choice of investments is set by the index. Investors benefit by an overall rise in the stock market and very low fees but may miss out on upticks in particular companies not included in the broad index.

GLOSSARY OF INVESTMENT TERMS

The following are common investment terms you might run across on your journey to financial freedom:

Ask: The seller's lowest acceptable sale price for an asset.

Asset: An investment capable of generating future income.

Balance sheet: An overall look at what a company owns as well as its liabilities and shareholder equity.

Bear market: A market on its way down.

Bid: The most a buyer is willing to pay for an investment.

Blue chip: A company with a long-standing proven record of stability.

Bond: An investment in a debt instrument of a company or government. Profits come from interest or price appreciation.

Broker: Someone paid to make investments for you.

Bull market: A market on its way up—the opposite of a bear market.

Capital gain (or loss): The cost to buy an investment minus what it sells for.

Cash-flow statement: A summary of inflows (typically income) and outflows (typically expenses) of cash in a household or business entity. While outflows are typically expense related, they can also consist of contributions to savings, loan principal payments, and prepaid expenses.

Diversity: A wide range of investments in one's portfolio.

Dividend: A portion of a company's income divided among shareholders.

Dollar Cost Averaging: Buying stock or other security for a fixed amount at set intervals resulting in a greater number of shares purchased when prices are low and a fewer number when high.

Liability: In the context of a balance sheet, a liability represents an obligation to pay. It can be any kind of debt, mortgage, or other promise to pay. Liabilities show up on a balance sheet as a subtraction from net worth.

Margin: Borrowed money, typically credit from a broker, used to make an investment.

Nasdaq Stock Market: The second largest stock exchange in the world.

New York Stock Exchange (NYSE): The world's largest stock exchange representing companies around the world.

Registered Investment Advisor (RIA): A financial investment advisor registered with state and federal regulators.

Stock: An investment representing ownership in a company.

Yield: The ratio between stock price paid and dividend paid. Also refers to the ratio of the interest paid on bonds and debt instruments to the principle amount.

For a more comprehensive list of terms, check out: www. investopedia.com/dictionary/

Acknowledgments

If I were to mention all of those who have inspired and motivated me over the years, it would take up half of the pages of this book. If you are not listed by name, please understand that I appreciate all the people I have interacted with over the years—most of you know who you are, and for those who don't, I will hopefully be able to express my gratitude in person.

I've been blessed with many things in life, beginning with the example of a strong work ethic provided by my mom, dad, and brothers. Growing up on a farm teaches one many things about life, and I'm forever indebted to my family for showing me the value of hard work, perseverance, and innovation, even when I wasn't sure any of it would pay off. I carried this work ethic into the corporate world where I was rewarded with increasing levels of accountability and ultimate responsibility over an important function in human resources—namely, employee benefits—which led me to counsel people on the rarely straightforward subject of personal finance.

My mentor throughout my time working with employee benefits was C. Dean Woods, a man with the patience and personality to teach me what many in corporate America forget—we serve others, not ourselves. Emblazoned in my mind is an anecdote Dean shared with me to best describe what he believed we in human resources did best. In the film of *To Kill a Mockingbird*, there is a scene right after Atticus learns Tom Robinson has committed suicide in jail. Miss Maudie sits Jem and Scout down and explains to the children why their father defended a black man accused of assaulting a white woman, a man who was a cultural outcast of the time: "There are some men in this world who are born to do our unpleasant jobs for us—your father is one of them."

Directing and managing employee benefits, payroll, or human resources is not a glamorous job. The role is largely behind the scenes. No one commends you for doing a good job, because doing so is simply expected. As a senior manager, you are only beckoned when there's a problem or when changes must be made, and both scenarios can be unpleasant. Dean showed me by counsel, character, and example how we must always advocate for the right thing, even when company officials and employees don't agree with our approach.

A special thanks to Mick Owens and family for helping me to better understand the world of personal finance and how having a comprehensive financial plan is the bedrock of our personal financial health.

The spreadsheets used throughout this book were designed by Jon Wittwer at Vertex42.com, and I'm grateful that he allowed me to use them in this book. John has an excellent menu of spreadsheets for dozens of personal finance and small business applications available at his website—most are free. I encourage you to visit his site and explore the resources.

I'm indebted to all those behind-the-scenes people who helped me navigate the world of book publishing. Thanks to Rachel Weaver LaBar, Holly Foreman, and Barbara Boyd for helping me through the writing and designing process—without your help, this book would never have happened.

And finally, many thanks to my wife Linda. Her dedication to teaching children with special needs has really been a life mission more than a career. The ability to teach those with special needs is a gift few of us have, and she has taught me that not all of us hear, see, or learn in the same way, which proved to be an invaluable perspective while writing this book. Without her grace and patience with all my foibles, I would, frankly, be a mess. She has been the calm wisdom and prayer warrior I needed, just in time. Our journey together has been a blessing far beyond what I have could have ever imagined more than thirty-three years ago. Who would have thought that first phone call, a two-hour one, would have led to a lifetime of love and memories? We are living proof that blind dates work. My own words cannot adequately describe all she means to me during our time together, so instead I'll rely on those of one of the wisest men to ever live, Solomon:

"Who can find a virtuous wife? For her worth is far above rubies. The heart of her husband safely trusts her; so he will have no lack of gain. She does him good and not evil all the days of her life."

—PROVERBS 31:10–12

About the Author

CERTIFIED FINANCIAL PLANNER™ professional MARK BAIRD loves money—though not in the traditional sense.

As a financial adviser and coach, Mark Baird is fascinated with the world of personal finance. He loves creating plans that allow people to reach their goals, all the while steering them away from destructive choices and showing them the path to financial freedom.

Having completed Dave Ramsey's Financial Coach Master Training, he's equipped many people with the skills they need to live without the stress a poor financial outlook can bring.

Baird holds a bachelor's degree from Purdue University in land surveying and an MBA from Houston Baptist University. He and his wife reside in Tipton County, Ind., where the family spends weekends harvesting and selling popcorn grown on their land. Mark can be reached through his website www.RulestoRiches.com.

51870967R00102

Made in the USA
San Bernardino, CA
03 August 2017